Supporting identity, diversity and language in the early years

Supporting early learning

Series Editors: Vicky Hurst and Jenefer Joseph

The focus of this series is on improving the effectiveness of early education. Policy developments come and go, and difficult decisions are often forced on those with responsibility for young children's well-being. This series aims to help with these decisions by showing how developmental approaches to early education provide a sound and positive basis for learning.

Each book recognizes that children from birth to 6 years old have particular developmental needs. This applies just as much to the acquisition of subject knowledge, skills and understanding as to other educational goals such as social skills, attitudes and dispositions. The importance of providing a learning environment that is carefully planned to stimulate children's own active learning is also stressed.

Throughout the series, readers are encouraged to reflect on the education being offered to young children, through revisiting developmental principles and using them to analyse their observations of children. In this way, readers can evaluate ideas about the most effective ways of educating young children and develop strategies for approaching their practice in ways that offer every child a more appropriate education.

Supporting identity, diversity and language in the early years

Iram Siraj-Blatchford
and Priscilla Clarke

Open University Press
Maidenhead

Open University Press
McGraw-Hill Education
McGraw-Hill House
Shoppenhangers Road
Maidenhead
Berkshire
SL6 2QL

email: enquiries@openup.co.uk
world wide web: www.openup.co.uk

First Published 2000
Reprinted 2001, 2003 (twice)

Copyright © I. Siraj-Blatchford and P. Clarke, 2000

A catalogue record of this book is available from the British Library

ISBN   0 335 20435 X (hb)   0 335 20434 1 (pb)

Library of Congress Cataloging-in-Publication Data
Siraj-Blatchford. Iram.
     Supporting identity, diversity and language in the early years/
Iram Siraj-Blatchford and Priscilla Clarke.
        p.   cm. – (Supporting early learning)
     Includes bibliographical references and index.
     ISBN 0-335-20435-X (hardcover). – ISBN 0-335-20434-1 (pbk.)
        1. Early childhood education – Great Britain   2. Child care – Great Britain.
3. Language acquisition.   4. Multicultural education – Great Britain.
5. Educational equalization – Great Britain.   I. Clarke, Priscilla, 1943– .
II. Title.   III. Series.
     LB1139.3.G7S57   2000
     372.21 0941–dc21   99-41547
                                                                                         CIP

Typeset by Type Study, Scarborough
Printed and bound in Great Britain by Biddles Ltd, www.biddles.co.uk

Contents

Series editors' preface

This book is one of a series which will be of interest to all those concerned with the care and education of children from birth to 6 years old – child-minders, teachers and other professionals in schools, those who work in playgroups, private and community nurseries and similar institutions; governors, providers and managers. We also speak to parents and carers, whose involvement is probably the most influential of all for children's learning and development.

Our focus is on improving the effectiveness of early education. Policy developments come and go, and difficult decisions are often forced on all those with responsibility for young children's well-being. We aim to help with these decisions by showing how developmental approaches to young children's education not only accord with our fundamental educational principles, but provide a positive and sound basis for learning.

Each book recognizes and demonstrates that children from birth to 6 years old have particular developmental learning needs, and that all those providing care and education for them would be wise to approach their work developmentally. This applies just as much to the acquisition of subject knowledge, skills and understanding, as to other educational goals such as social skills, attitudes and dispositions. In this series, there are several volumes with a subject-based focus, and the main aim is to show how that can be introduced to young children within the framework of an integrated and developmentally appropriate curriculum, without losing its integrity as an area of knowledge in its own right. We also stress the importance of providing a learning environment which is carefully planned for children's own active learning.

Access for all children is fundamental to the provision of educational opportunity. We are concerned to emphasize anti-discriminatory approaches throughout, as well as the importance of recognizing that meeting special educational needs must be an integral purpose of curriculum development and planning. We see the role of play in learning as a central one, and one which also relates to all-round emotional, social and physical development. Play, along with other forms of active learning, is normally a natural point of access to the curriculum for each child at his or her particular stage and level of understanding. It is therefore an essential force in making equal opportunities in learning, intrinsic as it is to all areas of development. We believe that these two aspects, play and equal opportunities, are so important that we not only highlight them in each volume in this series, but we also include separate volumes on them as well. The present volume is one of those. The authors take a unique approach to the relationship between children's cultural and linguistic heritage, and the development of their identity, self-concept and self-esteem. They offer guidance on both why and how practitioners should take account of these, with special emphasis on the acquisition of both the mother tongue and English as an additional language.

Throughout this series, we encourage readers to reflect on the education being offered to young children, by revisiting the developmental principles which most practitioners hold, and using them to analyse their observations of the children. In this way, readers can evaluate ideas about the most effective ways of educating young children, and develop strategies for approaching their practice in ways which exemplify their fundamental educational beliefs, and offer every child a more appropriate education.

The authors of each book in the series subscribe to the following set of principles for a developmental curriculum:

Principles for a developmental curriculum

- Each child is an individual and should be respected and treated as such.
- The early years are a period of development in their own right, and education of young children should be seen as a specialism with its own valid criteria of appropriate practice.
- The role of the educator of young children is to engage actively with what most concerns the child, and to support learning through these preoccupations.

- The educator has a responsibility to foster positive attitudes in children to both self and others, and to counter negative messages which children may have received.
- Each child's cultural and linguistic endowment is seen as the fundamental medium of learning.
- An anti-discriminatory approach is the basis of all respect-worthy education, and is essential as a criterion for a developmentally appropriate curriculum (DAC).
- All children should be offered equal opportunities to progress and develop, and should have equal access to good quality provision. The concepts of multiculturalism and anti-racism are intrinsic to this whole educational approach.
- Partnership with parents should be given priority as the most effective means of ensuring coherence and continuity in children's experiences, and in the curriculum offered to them.
- A democratic perspective permeates education of good quality and is the basis of transactions between people.

Vicky Hurst and Jenefer Joseph

Acknowledgements

There are a number of people we would like to thank for their support in compiling this book. Thanks are due to Jenefer Joseph and Rosemary Milne for being such an inspiration to us and to Shona Mullen, our commissioning editor, who has been patient, enthusiastic and as always, deeply professional. Special thanks are due to Sally Abbott Smith of the FKA Multicultural Resource Centre and Liz Brooker for sharing the photographs and to the centres, children, staff and parents from whom we continue to learn so much.

Identity, self-esteem and learning

Figure 1.1 Young children need positive role models
Photograph: Sally Abbott Smith

In all of our modern multicultural societies, it is essential that children learn to respect other groups and individuals, regardless of difference. This learning must begin in the very earliest years of a child's education. In this book we identify the groups that are often disadvantaged due to the poor understanding many early years staff have of them. We argue that there is a need to challenge the hidden oppression that is often imposed upon particular individuals and groups. While most early childhood settings appear to be calm and friendly places on the surface, we argue that there may be a great deal of underlying inequality. This may occur through differential policies, interactions, displays, or through variations in the curriculum or programme that the staff offer to some individuals or groups. These are important issues to be considered because they concern the early socialization of all of our children. In the early years children are very vulnerable and every adult, and other children as well, have the power to affect each child's behaviour, actions, intentions and beliefs.

Article 2 (1) of the UN Convention on the Rights of the Child (1989) states that:

1. The States Parties to the present Convention shall respect and ensure the rights set forth in the Convention to each child within their jurisdiction without discrimination of any kind, irrespective of the child's or his or her parents' or legal guardians' race, colour, sex, language, religion, political or other opinion, national, ethnic or social origin, property, disability, birth or other status.

2. States Parties shall take all appropriate measures to ensure that the child is protected against all forms of discrimination or punishment on the basis of the status, activities, expressed opinions, or beliefs of the child's parents, legal guardians or family members.

We aim to explore the ways in which children can be disadvantaged on the grounds of diversity in ethnic background, language, gender and socio-economic class in both intentional and in unintentional ways. The structures through which inequity can be perpetuated or measured are related to societal aspects such as employment, housing or education. For instance, we know that women earn less than men, as a group, and that working-class people live in poorer homes. We are concerned with the structural inequalities that create and support an over-representation of some groups in disadvantaged conditions. However, we do caution against the assumption that all members of a structurally oppressed group, for example, *all girls* are necessarily oppressed by those members of a structurally dominant group, for example, all boys. Because of the interplay between social class, gender, ethnicity and disability, identities are multifaceted. We therefore argue that children can hold contradictory individual positions with respect to the structural position that their 'group' holds in society. Interactional contexts are also often highly significant.

We will end the chapter by identifying the salient features of effective and ineffective practice in challenging oppression and in promoting respect for children, for parents and for staff in early child care and education settings (Siraj-Blatchford 1996).

The complexity of identity

A number of authors have written about the origins of inequality, about the implications for practice, and the need for a truly inclusive pedagogy and curriculum in the early years (see Davies 1989; Lloyd and Duveen 1992; Siraj-Blatchford 1992, 1994a; Clarke 1993; Siraj-Blatchford and Siraj-Blatchford 1995). We argue here that children can only learn to be tolerant, challenge unfair generalizations and learn inclusiveness and positive regard for diversity if they see the adults around them doing the same. Children will often imitate adult behaviour whether it is positive or negative, but they need to learn to discuss what they already know, just as we do (Brown 1998).

The way children feel about themselves is not innate or inherited, it is learned. A number of researchers (Lawrence 1988; Siraj-Blatchford 1994a) have shown that positive self-esteem depends upon whether children feel that others accept them and see them as competent and worthwhile. Researchers have also shown the connection between academic achievement and self-esteem. Purkey (1970) correlates high self-esteem with high academic performance. Positive action to promote self-esteem should form an integral part of work with children and ought to be incorporated into the everyday curriculum. Roberts (1998) argues that the process by which all children develop their self-esteem and identity rests heavily upon the type of interactions and relationships people form with young children.

Identity formation is a complex process that is never completed. The effects of gender, class and other formative categories overlap, in often very complicated ways, to shape an individual's identity. While we do not attempt to discuss this complexity in detail in this book, it is important for practitioners to be aware of the nature of shifting and changing identities. No group of children or any individual should be essentialized (in other words, defined and bound within this definition as if it were impossible for any individual to escape this) and treated as having a homogeneous experience with others of their 'type'.

A number of publications related to the development of children's personal, social and emotional education provide very useful strategies for supporting the positive development of children's personal identities (Lang 1995; Roberts 1998), yet few writers relate this work specifically to ethnicity, language, gender or class. There is now a great deal of research evidence of racial, gender and class inequality at a structural level in education (DES 1985; MacPherson 1999). Concerning racial identity, culture and 'agency' (the interactions between individuals and groups) there is only an emerging literature, and most of this is about adolescent school children (Gillborn 1990). This is particularly interesting because issues of gender and class identities have received more attention over the years, but again with regard to older children (Willis 1977; Mahony 1985). It is in the field of cultural studies that most writing on racial identity has occurred and this has mainly been in the areas of media studies and literary criticism. Only very recently has the focus turned to education, but again this has been largely focused on older children or on students in higher education (Siraj-Blatchford 1996).

Working-class and minority ethnic children's poor academic performance has been well documented (DES 1985; Bernstein 1992), as has girls' performance in particular subjects (Lloyd 1987). The link between racism, sexism, class prejudice and underachievement has been thoroughly argued. However, if those who work with young children are able to undermine children's self-esteem (however unintentional this might be) through negative beliefs about children's ability due to their gender, religion, language or ethnicity, then we have to evaluate our actions very carefully.

A child may be classed, gendered or 'racialized' (language status is also important here) in more than one way. Stuart Hall (1992), for example, discusses not only the discourses of identity but also those of difference within ethnic groups. In the very act of identifying ourselves as one thing, we simultaneously distance ourselves from something else. In terms of race and ethnicity, Hall argues that there are often contradictions within these categories as well as between these and other categories such as sexuality, class and disability. The way we perceive identities is very much shaped by how they are produced and taken up through the practices of representation (Grossberg 1994).

Making use of the metaphor of a kaleidoscope in understanding identity based on a range of inequalities, Hall (1992) argues that there will be individual differences within any identity forming category, such as race. We want to argue this is equally true of language, gender and social class. In his example, '. . . black signifies a range of experiences, the act of representation becomes not just about decentering the subject but actually exploring the kaleidoscopic conditions of blackness' (1992: 21). Grossberg (1994) argues that this notion of the 'kaleidoscopic conditions of blackness' (and presumably gender or class) depends on how and where one is situated. For instance, in Britain, a Pakistani woman who is a first generation immigrant and working class, will have a different identity to her son who is second generation British–Pakistani, and has become a teacher. Their experiences will vary because of how others perceive the (kaleidoscopic) combination of ethnic background in relation to their gender, socio-economic status, dress, language and so forth. Mother and son will certainly not be treated by others in the same way but they might have some shared experiences. Similarly in Australia two families of Greek origin, one working-class and one middle-class might be treated differently by others because of the different combination of class and ethnic background. They might themselves, as families, have different expectations for the same reasons.

It is important to highlight the complexity of identity formation in children. To ignore it is to ignore the child's individuality. It illustrates why each minority ethnic child and every girl or disabled child does not perceive themselves in the same way. In fact, children from structurally disadvantaged groups often hold contradictory positions, which is why we might find in our classrooms black and other minority ethnic children who are very confident and academically successful in spite of the structural, cultural and interpersonal racism in society. Similarly, we will find working-class boys who do not conform to a stereotype and are caring and unaggressive and African–Caribbean boys who are capable and well behaved. We should not be surprised at any of this (Siraj-Blatchford 1996).

The sexism, racism and other inequalities in our society can explain why at a structural level certain groups of people have less power while others have more. But at the level of interaction and agency we should be critically aware of the danger of stereotyping and should focus on individual people. This is not to suggest that we should ignore structure, far from it, we need to engage in developing the awareness of children and staff through policies and practices that explain and counter group inequalities. We will turn to the point of practice later. What we are suggesting is that educators need to work from a number of standpoints to fully empower the children in their care. Children need to be educated to deal confidently and fairly with each other and with others in an unjust society (Siraj-Blatchford 1992, 1994a, 1996).

Recent research has focused on the under-sevens. Many educators have begun to ask how it is that young children who are in our care learn about and experience class bias, sexism and racism. We know that children pick up stereotypical knowledge and understanding from their environment and try to make their own meanings from this experience. Outside experiences can come from parental views, media images and the child's own perceptions of the way people in their own image are seen and treated. In the absence of strong and positive role models children may be left with a negative or a positive perception of people like themselves. This bias can start from birth.

Barbara Lloyd (1987) conducted a number of studies in the late 1970s and the 1980s which illustrated how sex biased behaviour by mothers towards babies and infants contributed toward the gender stereotyping of boys and girls. One of her most interesting studies was conducted with Caroline Smith. Both researchers observed mothers of firstborn 6-month-olds while they played with babies who were systematically presented to the mothers as either a boy or girl. The mothers responded stereotypically, using their preconceived ideas of how boys and girls should behave. A baby, when presented as a boy, was encouraged to play with a hammer and engage in vigorous activity. Conversely, when the same baby was presented as a girl it was offered a soft doll and praised for being pretty and clever. The mothers generally appeared to favour gross-motor movements for boys.

We know that by the age of 13 months boy infants engage in more large motor-movements while girls make more fine motor responses. As Lloyd puts it:

> The gender differences at thirteen months may reflect babies' experiences at six months which are shaped by mothers' social representations of gender. (I interpret the thirteen month olds gender differentiated toy choice and play styles as evidence that these children are beginning to construct a concept of gender, albeit in practical activity and with some help from their mothers.)
>
>   (1987: 148)

Many parents and staff conclude from children's behaviour that they are naturally different, without considering their own contribution to the children's socialization. Difference, therefore, is also a matter of social learning, as well as physiology. This has implications for practice and the kinds of activities to which we should make sure all children have access, regardless of their gendered or other previous experiences.

Early years educators are often inexperienced and lack the knowledge and understanding about how children take on these biases and about how to deal with these matters. They often display a profound sense of inadequacy when faced with sexism and racism from children (Walkerdine 1987). Yet it is entirely natural for children to repeat the behaviours to which they have been exposed by parents and other significant adults.

Dual heritage children's identity

The issue of identity formation becomes even more complex for children with more apparent multiple identities such as children from 'biracial' families. This is a poorly researched area and there is usually very little information to support parents or staff on their work with dual heritage children. In America these children are often referred to as biracial. Francis Wardle (1999) provides an illuminating account of being a white father raising his four biracial children with his spouse who is black. Both parents worked extremely hard to raise their children with a full dual heritage which included learning about their histories, their families and differing cultural backgrounds. Because he was unable to get the support and information he needed to do this when his children were little, he is now an author of several texts on the subject. Any reader who has concerns about biracial or dual heritage children should read the book, which contains many useful references and addresses. As he says, 'A biracial child raised with pride and acceptance of all parts of her heritage will easily function with Black and White children, and will have very wide tolerance for differences and diversity. She will not need to consider a child's racial label before she accepts him' (1999: 7). He goes on to add, 'When Kealan, our son, first attended middle school, several Black children accused him of trying to be White, trying to be better than them. Because Kealan knows his heritage includes his White relatives, he was not ashamed of being accused of being White – because he knows he partly is!' (1999: 7).

Staff need to find resources and a shared language with which to work with dual heritage children and their parents to support a strong identity. But it would be even better, and we would certainly advocate it, if staff worked with all children to make them aware that they *all* have an ethnic/racial identity and that they all have a linguistic, gendered, cultural and diverse identity. Surely this is the way forward? In being sure of ones' own identity as multi-faceted, it must be easier for children to accept that others are exactly the same – even when the combinations are different!

Identity and achievement

Cultural identity should be seen as a significant area of concern for curriculum development (Siraj-Blatchford 1996). All children and adults identify with classed, gendered and racialized groups (as well as other groups), but what is especially significant is that some cultural identities are seen as less 'academic' than others (often by the staff and children). We know that children can hold views about their 'masterful' or 'helpless' attributes as learners (Dweck and Leggett 1988). Dweck and Leggett (1988) therefore emphasize the importance of developing 'mastery' learning dispositions in children. There is evidence that children who experience education through taking some responsibility for their actions and learning become more effective learners. They are learning not only the content of the curriculum but the processes by which learning takes place (Siraj-Blatchford 1998). Roberts (1998) argues that the important area of personal and social education should be treated as a curriculum area worthy of separate activities, planning and assessment.

The 'helpless' views adopted by some children can be related to particular areas of learning and can lead to underachievement in a particular area of the curriculum. Children construct their identities in association with their perceived cultural heritage (Siraj-Blatchford 1996). Recently we have heard a good deal in the British press about (working-class) boys' underachievement. The results from the school league-tables suggest that some boys do underachieve in terms of basic literacy, but it is important to note that this is only certain groups of boys and not all boys. In the UK working-class white boys and African–Caribbean boys are particularly vulnerable. Similarly, children from some minority ethnic groups perform poorly in significant areas of the curriculum while other minority ethnic groups achieve particularly highly (Gillborn and Gipps 1997).

It is apparent that certain confounding identities, for instance, white/working-class/male, can lead to lower outcomes because of expectations held by the children and adults. In asserting their masculinity, white working-class boys might choose gross-motor construction activities over reading or pre-reading activities. Similarly, some girls may identify more strongly with home-corner play and favour nurturing activities over construction choices. Class, gender and ethnicity are all complicit here and the permutations are not simple, but they do exist and do lead to underachievement. The answer is to avoid essentializing children's identities but also requires educators to take an active role in planning for, supporting and developing individual children's identities as masterful learners of a broad and balanced curriculum (Siraj-Blatchford 1998).

As previously suggested, in the active construction of their identities, children distance themselves from 'others' (Siraj-Blatchford and Siraj-Blatchford 1999). As one little boy was overheard in a playgroup saying to another boy, 'Why do you just sit reading? Girls read, boys play football!' The issue is therefore to show children that they are mistaken in associating these 'others' with particular areas of learning. We have to extend children's identity as learners and break down the stereotypes. Boys need to disassociate literacy from 'girls' stuff, and be presented with strong male role models that value literacy. It is in this context that we can see the

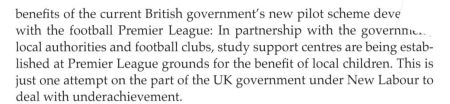

benefits of the current British government's new pilot scheme deve
with the football Premier League: In partnership with the governme...
local authorities and football clubs, study support centres are being established at Premier League grounds for the benefit of local children. This is
just one attempt on the part of the UK government under New Labour to
deal with underachievement.

Diversity, equity and learning

Four main conditions need to be satisfied for learning to take place, the
second two will be dealt with in subsequent chapters, but we want to
argue here that we need an understanding of the first two to lay the foundations for learning:

- the child needs to be in a state of emotional well-being and secure;
- the child needs a positive self-identity and self-esteem;
- the curriculum must be social/interactional and instructive;
- the child needs to be cognitively engaged.

It is widely recognized that an integrated, holistic and developmental
approach is needed to learning, teaching and care with children from birth
to 7. Many adults believe children remain innocent, but even the very
youngest children are constantly learning from what and who is around
them. They learn not only from what we intend to teach but from all of
their experiences. For example, if girls and boys or children from traveller
families are treated differently or in a particular manner from other people
then children will learn about the difference as part of their world-view. To
deny this effect is to deny that children are influenced by their socialization. The need for emotional, social, physical, moral, aesthetic and mental
well-being all go hand in hand.

The early years curriculum should therefore incorporate work on children's awareness of similarities and differences, and to help them to see
this as 'normal'. For instance, research evidence produced by David
Milner (1983) has shown that children have learned positive and negative
feelings about racial groups from an early age. Milner suggests that children as young as three demonstrate an awareness of a racial hierarchy
'in line with current adult prejudices' (1983: 122). Some children can be
limited in their development by their view that there are people around
them who do not value them because of who they are. This would suggest
that early years staff need to offer *all* children guidance and support in
developing positive attitudes towards all people. A focus on similarities
is as important as dealing with human differences (see Siraj-Blatchford

and MacLeod-Brudenell 1999). The early years is an appropriate time to develop this work with young children.

In Siraj-Blatchford (1994a: 45) reference was made to a boy who was (re)named Amar for the purposes of publication. Amar was 3½ years old when he announced, 'I'm not putting my wellies in that bag, it's got Paki writing on it.' Amar had already learnt to recognize the difference between English script and the script of his mother tongue. He had learnt that there are different languages with different scripts, and that these languages are valued by different people. Tragically, he had also decided even at that tender age that the people who really seemed to matter thought little of his home language and that he should reject it as well. Amar is not an isolated example, and for every one minority ethnic child who learns to look down upon majority world languages, there are countless more monolingual children who do the same.

How do young children who are in our care experience and learn about social class or linguistic prejudice, sexism or racism? How does this effect their learning more generally? These are questions that staff need to address. We know that children adopt biased (both good and bad) knowledge and understanding from their environment. This can be from parental views, media images, and the child's own perceptions of the way people are seen and treated. The most common form of prejudice young children experience is through name-calling or through negative references by other children (or adults) to their gender, dress, appearance, skin colour, language or culture. Educators may hear some of these remarks and it is vital that these are dealt with appropriately as they arise. The following childlike remarks have deep consequences for the children who utter them, and for those receiving them:

'You're brown so you're dirty.'
'Girls can't play football.'
'Don't be a sissy.'
'Boys can't skip.'
'She's got dirty clothes.'

Early years educators are often worried about their lack of experience and their lack of knowledge and understanding in dealing with these matters. They often display a profound sense of inadequacy when faced with prejudice from children. They may also doubt whether name-calling is wrong and they might even see it as 'natural behaviour' (Siraj-Blatchford 1994a).

In a study on playground behaviour, Ross and Ryan (1990) highlight findings about sexist and racist name-calling and stereotyping during playtime. Grugeon and Woods' (1990) ethnographic study of primary schools identified a number of the effects of racism upon the self-images of South Asian children. Children were seen colouring themselves pink, describing themselves as having blue eyes and fair hair, they refused to go out into the sun in case they became brown(er), and avoided participation in minority ethnic festivals.

Troyna and Hatcher's (1991) study showed that while racism is a commonplace feature in the lives of most minority ethnic children, many of the majority ethnic children who perpetuate this racism have egalitarian attitudes that educators need to engage with. As Troyna and Hatcher say:

> Many children display inconsistent and contradictory repertoires of attitudes, containing both elements of racially egalitarian ideologies and elements of racist ideologies ... [and] ... a number of combinations of attitudes and behaviour is possible, ranging from children who hold racist beliefs but do not express them in their behaviour, to children who hold racially egalitarian beliefs but use racist name-calling in certain situations.
>
> (1991: 197)

A number of studies have also drawn attention to the verbal abuse directed at minority ethnic children by other minority ethnic children (Grugeon and Woods 1990). While Grugeon and Woods call for further research to study what they consider 'minorities among minorities', we would argue along with Troyna and Hatcher (1991) that these cases actually provide evidence of children simply 'trading' on commonly held and expressed racist ideologies without necessarily believing in them. We could argue from this evidence that children might also be trading insults across gender and class boundaries in the same way.

Children in all types of early childhood settings might have similar experiences. Students, teachers, childminders and playgroup workers have often asked how they can deal with class, gender and ethnic prejudice. The first step is to recognize that the problem exists. As Davey (1983) has argued, we have to accept that a system of racial categorization and classification exists and that, until it is finally rejected by everyone, it will continue to provide an irresistible tool by which children can simplify and make meaning of their social world. It would be a great mistake to assume that this is only a 'problem' in largely multi-ethnic settings. Strategies which allow children to discuss, understand and deal with oppressive behaviour aimed at particular groups such as: minority ethnic children, girls, the disabled and younger children are essential in all settings. We suggest that educators should always make opportunities for stressing similarities as well as differences.

Promoting positive self-esteem

Early childhood educators have an instrumental role to play in this development. Staff need to help children learn to guide their own behaviour in a way that shows respect and caring for themselves, other children and adults, and their immediate and the outside environment. Values education goes hand-in-hand with good behaviour management practices. The way that adults and children relate to each other in any setting is an indication of the ethos of that setting. To create a positive ethos for equity practices, staff in every setting will need to explore what the ethos in their setting feels like to the users, such as parents, children and staff. Staff need to explore what behaviours, procedures and structures create the ethos, what aspects of the existing provision is positive and which is negative, and who is responsible for change.

Children need help from the adults around them in learning how to care for each other and to share things. To help the children in this respect, the educator must have the trust of the children and their parents. Young children's capacity to reflect and see things from another person's point of view is not fully developed. Most small children find it difficult to see another person's view as equally important. Children need a lot of adult guidance to appreciate the views and feelings of others. This can be learnt from a very early age. In her research on the relationship between mothers and their babies, and relationships between very young siblings, Judy Dunn (1987) suggests that mothers who talk to their children about 'feeling states' have children who themselves 'become particularly articulate about and interested in feeling states' (1987: 38). Consideration for others has to be learnt.

We believe that children need educators who will consciously:

- encourage positive interactions;
- encourage discussion about how they and others feel;
- encourage attention to other points of view;
- encourage communication with others;
- try to ensure that they learn constructive ways to resolve differences;
- promote cooperation, not competition.

(Adapted from Stonehouse 1991: 78)

Of course educators cannot expect children to behave in this way if they do not practise the same behaviour themselves. If children see us showing kindness, patience, love, empathy, respect and care for others, they are more likely to want to emulate such behaviour. For many educators the experience of working actively with children in this way may be underdeveloped, especially when it comes to dealing with incidents of sexism or racism. Each setting, as part of their equity policy will need to discuss the issue of harassment and devise procedures for dealing with it. According to Siraj-Blatchford (1994a) staff can take some of the following actions in dealing with incidents of name-calling:

Short-term action

- If you hear sexist, racist or other remarks against other people because of the ethnicity, class or disability you should not ignore them or you will be condoning the behaviour and therefore complying with the remarks.
- As a 'significant other' in the children's lives, they are likely to learn from your value position. Explain clearly why the remarks made were wrong and hurtful or offensive, and ask the abused children and the abusers how they felt so that the children can begin to think actively about the incident.
- Do not attack the children who have made the offending remarks in a personal manner or imply that the children are wrong, only that what was said is wrong.
- Explain in appropriate terms to the abusers why the comment was wrong, and give all the children the correct information.
- Support and physically comfort the abused children, making sure that they know that you support their identity and that of their group and spend some time working with them on their activity.
- At some point during the same day, work with the children who made the offending remarks to ensure that they know that you continue to value them as people.

Long-term action

- Target the parents of children who make offensive discriminatory comments to ensure that they understand your policy for equality, and that you will not accept abuse against any child. Point out how this damages their child.
- Develop topics and read stories which raise issues of similarities and differences in language, gender and ethnicity and encourage the children to talk about their understandings and feelings.
- Create the kind of ethos that promotes and values diverse images and contributions to society.
- Involve parents and children (depending on the age of the children) in decision-making processes, particularly during the development of a policy on equality.
- Talk through your equality policy with all parents as and when children enter the setting, along with the other information parents need.

- Develop appropriate teaching and learning strategies for children who are acquiring English so that they do not get bored, frustrated and driven to poor behaviour patterns.

(Adapted from Siraj-Blatchford 1994a)

Working towards effective practice

The identity (or ethos) of the early childhood setting is very important (Suschitzky and Chapman 1998). We identify six stages of equity oriented practice, stage one being the least desirable and least developed practice in the area. These are based on our own and other colleagues' experiences within and observations of a very wide range of early years settings. The six stages are not meant to be prescriptive or definitive, but they are intended to stimulate discussion and thought among early years staff and parents. Different kinds of beliefs and practices are identified that promote or hinder the implementation of equity practices that allow children, parents and staff to feel either valued or devalued.

Stage 1

Discriminatory practice – where diversity according to gender, class, ability or cultural and racial background is seen as a disadvantage and a problem, and no effort has been made to explore positive strategies for change. There is a separatist, or overtly racist, sexist and/or classist environment. We may observe some of the following:

- Staff believe that all children are 'the same' and that sameness of treatment is sufficient regardless of a child's gender, social class, special needs or ethnicity.
- Staff believe that no extra resources are required to meet needs based on difference.
- Parents are blamed for children not 'fitting in' to the way the setting functions and that if parents are dissatisfied with the service they should take their children elsewhere.
- Inflexible curriculum and assessment procedures which do not reflect a recognition for the need for positive minority ethnic or gender role models, multilingualism in society or sufficient observations that detect special needs.
- Staff avoid providing parents who might have difficulty with English with information in any language other than English.
- Staff have little or no understanding of issues of inequality, such as poverty, gender, racial or disability stereotyping.

- There are no policy statement of intent or policy documents relating to equal opportunities. British culture, child rearing patterns, etc., are universalized.
- Staff believe English is the only medium which is appropriate for use in the early childhood setting.

Stage 2

Inadequate practice – where children's special needs are recognized according to disability but generally a deficit model exists. If children who perform poorly also happen to be from a minority ethnic group this is seen as contributory. Gendered reasons may be given for poor achievement. Alternatively the parents are blamed for being inadequate at parenting. We may observe some of the following:

- There is a general acceptance that staff are doing their best without actually undertaking staff development for equality issues except for special needs.
- It is recognized that extra resources should be provided for children with English as an additional language, but it is felt that this is a special need which should be met by an English as an Additional Language (EAL) teacher or assistant, and that 'these' children will find it difficult to learn until they have acquired a basic grasp of English.
- Staff withdraw children with EAL for 'special English groups', implying that learning EAL is different from other learning.
- Staff encourage children to play with a range of resources but no special effort is being made to encourage girls to construct or boys to play in the home corner.
- Staff do not know how to, or do not want to, challenge discriminatory remarks because they feel the children pick these up from home, and they do not feel they can raise these issues with parents.
- Staff may direct parents to provide interpreters.

Stage 3

Well meaning but poorly informed practice – where staff are keen to meet individual children's needs and are receptive to valuing diversity. We may observe some of the following:

- Token measures at valuing diversity can be observed, for example, multilingual posters, black dolls and puzzles and books with positive black and gender role models may be found but are rarely the focus of attention.

- There is an equal opportunities policy statement but this does not permeate other documents related to parent guides, curriculum or assessment.
- Staff respond positively to all parents and children and appreciate diversity as richness but are not well informed about their cultures or about anti-racist, sexist or classist practice.
- Staff provide a thematic approach 'Greek week', 'Chinese New Year' without recognizing that diversity should be reflected across the curriculum.
- Bilingual staff are employed as extra 'aides' or 'assistants'.
- Staff development consists of occasional individual attendance at equal opportunities and special needs conferences and workshops but these are not disseminated to all staff.

Stage 4

Practice that values diversity generally where some attempts are made to provide an anti-discriminatory curriculum and environment. We may observe some of the following:

- There is a centre policy on equal opportunities which includes promoting gender, race and other equality issues.
- Parents are respected and staff assume that minority ethnic parents have a lot to offer.
- Staff are inhibited through worries about parents raising objections to anti-racist or anti-sexist practice.
- Staff are aware of inequality issues related to their profession and the under-representation of male and black educators.
- Resources are applied which promote anti-discriminatory work and special activities to promote racial harmony and gender and race equality are practised. All children are observed carefully to detect any special learning needs.
- Children's home languages are valued and attempts are made to encourage parents to support bilingualism at home.

Stage 5

Practice that values diversity and challenges discrimination, where equal opportunities is firmly on the agenda. We may observe some of the following:

- The centre staff have made a conscious effort to learn about inequality through staff development and someone is allocated with responsibility for promoting good practice in the area.

- There is a policy statement on equal opportunities and a document which applies the statement of intent to everyday practice, curriculum evaluation and assessment and to the positive encouragement of anti-discriminatory activities.
- Staff observe the children's learning and interactions with equality in mind and develop short- and long-term plans to promote self-image, self-esteem, language and cultural awareness.
- Festivals are celebrated and the centre ethos uses a range of multi-cultural, multifaith and multilingual resources.
- Staff are keen to challenge stereotypes and confident to raise issues with parents and support them through their learning if they hold negative stereotypes.
- Bilingual staff are employed as mainstream staff.
- Staff do not tolerate racial, gender or disability harassment and have agreed procedures for dealing with any such incidents.
- Staff value the community they work in and encourage parents to be involved in decision making.

Stage 6

Challenging inequality and promoting equity, where staff actively try to change the structures and power relations which inhibit equal opportunities. We may observe some of the following:

- The centre staff have made a conscious effort to learn about inequality through staff development and someone is allocated with responsibility for promoting good practice in the area.
- Staff value the community they work in and encourage parents to be involved in decision making. Bi/multi-lingualism is actively supported.
- The management take full responsibility for promoting equal opportunities and try positively to promote their service to all sections of the community.
- Management actively seek to recruit more male and minority ethnic staff.
- The equal opportunities policy is monitored and evaluated regularly and staff are confident in their anti-discriminatory practice.
- Equality issues are reflected across curriculum, resources, assessment and record keeping and the general ethos of the centre.
- Staff are non-judgemental and do not universalize English-speaking as best, they value a range of family forms, cultures and child-rearing practices.
- Parents and children are supported against discrimination in the local community.
- Staff know how to use the UK Sex Discrimination Act, Race Relations

Act, the Warnock Report, Code of Practice, the Children Act and the United Nations Convention on the Rights of Children to achieve equality assurance.

• Staff take a proactive approach to racism outside their own centre.
• Centre staff share their knowledge and expertise with others.

(Adapted from Siraj-Blatchford 1996)

A positive self concept is necessary for healthy development and learning and includes feelings about gender, race, ability, culture and language. Positive self-esteem depends on whether children feel that others accept them and see them as competent and worthwhile. Young children develop attitudes about themselves and others from a very early age and need to be exposed to positive images of diversity in the early years setting. Children need to feel secure and to learn to trust the staff that care for them in order to learn effectively.

Further reading

Lloyd, B. and Duveen, G. (1992) *Gender Identities and Education: The Impact of Starting School*. London: Harvester Wheatsheaf.

Siraj-Blatchford, I. (1994) *The Early Years: Laying the Foundations for Racial Equality*. Stoke-on-Trent: Trentham Books.

Wardle, F. (1999) *Tomorrow's Children: Meeting the Needs of Multiracial and Multiethnic Children at Home, in Early Childhood Programs and at School*. Denver, CO: Center for the Study of Biracial Children.

Yelland, N. (ed.) (1998) *Gender in Early Childhood*. London: Routledge.

2

Language acquisition and diversity

Figure 2.1 Talking about books and stories is fun!
Photograph: Sally Abbott Smith

There is no doubt about the importance that language plays in the lives of children. Language involves more than learning a linguistic code with which to label the world or to refer to abstract concepts; language also involves learning how to use the code in socially appropriate and effective ways. It is not just a question of learning the words and grammar of another language, you must also know how to use them in socially acceptable ways. The specific values, beliefs and relationships which comprise the social life of the group whose language the child is learning, shape the patterns of language usage in that community in complex and important ways (Schieffelin and Ochs 1986). Thus young children grow up learning their first language or languages through the social life of their own communities, they learn the values, beliefs and roles through their interactions with a number of different community members. As they grow up they learn to function as competent members of speakers of that language.

Language develops rapidly in the early years and all children, including those who come from language backgrounds other than English, benefit from good quality programmes which emphasize interaction and the development of communication skills. It is clear that the best programmes build on children's individual needs, interests and identities.

Language acquisition

Defining language is a complex task. Gonzales-Mena (1998: 324) defines language as 'the formation and communication of information, thoughts and feelings through the use of words'. Language learning is dependent on cognition. The main features of language are listening, speaking, reading and writing. However, non-verbal language and the language of media also need to be included.

All children acquire a first language regardless of what that language is. Babies are ready to listen and pay attention to the voices of their parents and caregivers from the first days after birth. This is strengthened through social interaction within the family.

Acquiring a first language is a complex task. A language system is a puzzle with a variety of interlocking pieces: *phonology* (the sounds of the language); *vocabulary* (the words of the language); *grammar* (the way the words are ordered and put together); *discourse* (the way the sentences are put together); and *pragmatics* (the rules of how to use the language) Tabors (1997: 7).

Young children are considered to be competent in using the language when they have mastered all these pieces. This is a major task for children in the first six years. The process of language development begins with the development of sounds and babbling. Initially babies are able to make a variety of sounds. By the end of the first year of life, babies can associate talk with the facial expressions of speakers, they can produce a variety of sounds that match those in their home environment or the environment they spend most time in, they can recognize the intonations of familiar people, they can take turns in conversation with adults, they can use gestures to indicate their needs, and they can respond in socially appropriate ways (Makin, Campbell and Jones Diaz 1995: 6–7).

Between 12 and 18 months, many babies can produce first words or units of language. The first vocabulary of young children usually contains the names of people and objects, functional words such as 'no', 'mine', 'up' and 'gone' and social routines such as 'bye-bye'. After acquiring single words, children begin to show an understanding of the early grammatical requirements of language by putting these single words together to make small sentences which express more complex relationships. This is sometimes called 'telegraphic speech'. Sometimes the same words or groups of words will have different meanings as the following example shows:

Anna (15 months old): Milk *(holds up bottle).*
Caregiver: You've finished your milk? Do you want some more?
Anna: Up.
Caregiver: No more? You want to get out of the chair?

Just like parents, caregivers can interpret the requests of young children even if their language is restricted. At the same time as they are beginning to put words together, babies and toddlers are beginning to take part in interactive routines with parents and caregivers. These routines provide practice with turn-taking.

The major types of complex sentences emerge between the ages of about 2 and 4 years. Children in the early years are beginning to learn the rules of the language. On the basis of these rules they can produce and understand an infinite set of sentences. However, they will still make mistakes when they speak. They will say 'foots' instead of 'feet' and 'goed' instead of 'went'. These words are over-generalizations of rules that children are extracting from the language that they hear. However, children as old as 8 or 9 years of age are still working out complicated word meanings.

A major part of the development of the language of children in the 3 to 6 age group is the ability to construct conversations. Children are by then beginning to develop arguments and to tell narratives. This includes conversations with older children and adults who strengthen the child's ability to ask and answer questions. At the same time as children are learning the grammar of their language they are also learning the social and cultural ways of language. As they take part in conversations, children learn the rules for turn-taking, they learn different ways of talking for different occasions and they begin to learn formal and informal ways of addressing different people. By 4 years of age children have learned to adjust their speech to different audiences.

In the following example the teacher is talking to Winsome (aged 4 years) and Tanya (4 years) about the way babies talk.

Teacher: If you were pretending to be a little baby, how would you talk?

Winsome: You couldn't.

Teacher: But if you were just learning to talk.

Tanya: Sometimes I'd say this – br br br.

Teacher: Would that be like a baby learning to talk? How does Nicky talk?

Tanya: (*in a squeaky voice*) She says hello hello. She says mum mum and ya ya.

Teacher: What's that?

Tanya: That's my name, my name is princess – she calls me ya ya.

Winsome: I'd say mummy mummy aah aah aah (*she laughs*) that's what babies say.

Clarke (1976)

When young children who speak a home language other than English start in the nursery or pre-school setting they begin the process of learning an additional language. Some of these children already speak more than one language. However, suddenly the language that they have used for their daily lives is no longer the language that they hear around them. They are surrounded by a new language and an environment which is also unfamiliar. Unless early childhood educators are familiar with the children's home language, social class background and culture, and provide a supportive environment, these children are in danger of being marginalized and may experience an insecure and anxious start to their entry into nursery and schooling.

A good quality early childhood programme can foster rich language interactions for all children and it can support and maintain the first or home languages of bilingual children as well. It is therefore important for children learning English as an additional language to be exposed to their new language within the quality early childhood programme rather than to be withdrawn from their peers and taught English through direct instruction.

The importance of interaction

If children remain at home until they are 3 or 4 years of age, the basis of their language is learned by being immersed in their home environment and by conversing with other family members. The children are learning about the meaning and function of language through everyday acts such as giving and receiving instructions, talking on the telephone and talking together at meal times.

When children enter nursery or school most have already gained the basis of their language development but for some the language that they know and use at home is not the same as the one used in their new environment of the nursery or school. This means that they now have to learn new vocabulary and new ways of communicating. In the early months of their English language learning in the nursery or school, those children with a different home language learn to tie new words to concepts learned through their first language. They must also learn to transfer knowledge of the way language has worked for them in the home setting to the new environment of the early childhood setting. These children have the potential to become bilingual if they are given opportunities to use their home languages in the new setting and to learn new names for objects and actions already learned through their first language.

In the early years, interaction with adults and other children is the key to acquisition of language. For infants and toddlers their early interactions with parents and caregivers provide the basis for communication and learning in both the first or home language and in second language acquisition. These early infant–caregiver interactions establish a basis for communication and continue to be the context for the development of the child's language throughout the early years (Trevarthen 1992).

Language and thought

Researchers such as Vygotsky (1962, 1978) and Bruner (1983, 1990a,b) have argued that language plays a greater role in facilitating thought than Piaget (1962) recognized. Their work demonstrates the important two-way relationship between language development and the social context in supporting interaction in the early years.

Vygotsky's (1962, 1978) theory is built on the fundamental premise that development occurs on the social level within a cultural context, and language is the major tool by which adults induct children into a particular view of the world. According to Vygotsky, social experiences shape the way individuals think and interpret the world.

Vygotsky viewed the acquisition of language as a major milestone in children's cognitive development. His theories underpin the importance of talk between children and adults, and between children and children, for cognitive development. Bruner (1975, 1983, 1990 a,b); Vygotsky (1978) and Wells (1981) have all stressed the importance of language in terms of its use as a tool of social interaction as well as a tool for organizing knowledge. They argue that language plays a major role in facilitating thought, emphasizing the two-way relationship between language development and the social context.

For staff and children in the early years, Vygotsky's (1978) notion of The Zone of Proximal Development (ZPD) has proved useful. The ZPD represents the gap between what children understand or can do alone and what they can do with assistance from an older person or more experienced peer. According to Vygotsky, this is the area where, with the help of an adult, children can go beyond their present development. Furthermore, the effective adult subtly modifies each consequent interaction so that the learner gradually takes over responsibility for the learning. Vygotsky's theory of the way that the adult can build 'scaffolding' or 'bridges' to help the child progress is important for understanding the way staff can assist children learning a second language.

Bruner (1983) emphasized that language is acquired through active use, rather than by merely being exposed to it. He emphasized the role of an adult in assisting a child achieve what is not possible alone. The following example shows the way the teacher scaffolds the learning of a 4-year-old English as an additional language learner.

> *Child (4 years):* Judy, this where? (*Holds a piece of puzzle up and points to the puzzle*).
> *Teacher:* Where do you want to put that piece?
> *Child:* A cat.
> *Teacher:* You're making a puzzle about a cat.
> *Child:* A eye.
> *Teacher:* Yes that's right. It might fit here (*she points to the place where it will fit*).
> *Child:* One more eye.
> *Teacher:* That's right. It's got two eyes. Somewhere near the other one? Oh good shot (*the teacher nods her head as the child tries to fit the piece in*).
>
> Clarke (1996)

The scaffolding used by the teacher (Judy) encourages a high level of child involvement and the strategies she uses include: demonstrating and modelling, identifying problems, turn-taking, questioning, cueing the learner in, paying attention to repetition and praising efforts. Her scaffolding has provided contextual clues for the child, including the use of visual support and non-verbal gestures such as pointing.

Elliott (1994: 9) has identified the following characteristics of scaffolding; making instructional goals explicit, actively monitoring learner progress, providing immediate and educationally oriented feedback, and creating an environment that is task oriented but relaxed. In addition, other characteristics of scaffolding should include providing social, cultural and linguistic relevance.

Social competence

One of the most important challenges for early childhood workers is to help children develop the skills to interact with others. Developing the social skills that assist children to get along with their peers and adults will have a significant impact on their lives. Sebastian-Nickell and Milne (1992: 126) suggest that the development of social competence is a life-long process that begins in the first few weeks of the child's life. This process can be supported by parents and by early childhood staff. Young children need support to develop interactive skills in one-to-one and in group situations. Even at this level, language is a major tool.

Social skills involve the strategies we use when interacting with others. They cover awareness of feelings of others. Social skills are used to enter and maintain interactions, to engage others in conversation, to maintain friendships and to cope with conflict. Non-verbal skills involve smiling, nodding, eye contact and the development of listening skills. All of these non-verbal strategies form foundations for language interactions.

Children under 3 years

In the first six months, babies smile and respond to sounds made by familiar people and react to familiar situations. According to Trevarthen (1992) babies actually initiate interaction and response from others, especially their parents. Between 6 months and 12 months, babies observe and imitate others, are possessive about their own toys, babble and begin to make sounds. From 1 to 2 years, toddlers are becoming aware of their feelings, enjoy solitary and parallel play and have difficulty sharing. They are also beginning to show assertiveness, independence and interest in the world around them. By 2 to 3 years of age, children are aware of their emotions, show their feelings in various ways, play well alongside others, need adult approval, enjoy symbolic play and imitating others, and like to please.

All babies and toddlers in childcare and nursery settings need opportunities for warm interactions with adults. Young children need consistency in the care provided, and those children who come from language backgrounds other than English need support from staff who speak their first or home languages on a consistent basis. The children need to receive messages that say they are important to their caregivers. They need to develop a feeling of trust in their new environment. Staff need to respect all the children in their care. This means taking particular care to understand and acknowledge the different cultural and socio-economic backgrounds of the children and make special efforts to work with families to assist the children to settle into a new environment.

Boys and girls can have different language experiences within the same household. Dunn (1987) studied the relationship between mothers' conversation styles with their children aged 18–24 months. She states:

> The analysis also showed marked and consistent differences in the frequency of such conversations in families with girls and with boys. Mothers talked more to 18-month-old daughters about feeling states than they did to their 18-month-old sons. By 24 months the daughters themselves talked more about feeling states than did the sons.
>
> (1987: 37)

In multicultural or diverse societies there is a great variety of family values and traditions and it is important that children are brought up to balance the tensions and handle the adjustments of being reared in one way and being educated in another. Children need to become socialized into the new practices and society. Early childhood staff need to be patient, caring, tolerant, flexible and need to be able to communicate effectively with parents and other staff about their work.

Sebastian-Nickell and Milne (1992: 126) suggest 12 ways that early childhood staff can foster social competence by:

- helping to build trust;
- responding appropriately to individual differences in temperaments;
- helping children learn house rules;
- helping children learn to cooperate and accept responsibility in helping;
- creating a physical environment that fosters small group activities and interests;
- helping children learn how to share and take turns;
- helping children to develop successful relationships with peers;

- helping children to be assertive, not aggressive;
- helping children develop a sense of regard for the well being of others;
- helping children to seek assistance when appropriate and to use early childhood staff as a resource;
- helping children develop skills in solving interpersonal problems;
- recognizing that different cultures have different social practices.

When 2½-year-old Amy entered the nursery, staff were concerned that she seemed so upset by the strange environment; by the fact no one could speak her language (Cantonese) and also that her mother seemed upset that Amy was clinging to her. The staff had already learned that Amy had only just arrived from Hong Kong after living with her grandparents while the parents tried to get established in Australia. Through an interpreter, Amy's mother explained that she would only be able to stay for the morning as she was working and her employer had said she could not take much free time. The nursery did not have a Cantonese speaker but a local resource agency was able to provide short-term bilingual support for the first few weeks. The staff in consultation with the mother and the interpreter put together a strategy for supporting Amy's settlement into the nursery. The strategy developed for Amy included:

- a session with the educator, the parents and the interpreter to fill in the bilingual enrolment form;
- a session with the staff in the toddler room, the mother and the interpreter, to discuss Amy's usual routines at home, where she slept, her favourite toy, the languages used, any allergies or food preferences;
- an arrangement with the mother or father to bring Amy a little later each day when the other children were settled and for a parent to remain with her for a short time;
- for the parent to provide familiar food for her lunch each day;
- for the parent to bring Amy's toy that she sleeps with;
- for one staff in the nursery to be the 'significant' caregiver when Amy arrived each day;
- for a bilingual support worker to attend the nursery for the first three days and then attend on single days over the next four weeks.

Over the next few days, Amy gradually learned the routines of the centre and the staff used intervention strategies to assist Amy to mix with other children.

In order to foster social interaction, adults who provide a good example of collaborative and cooperative practices and who facilitate a programme that acknowledges culture, language, gender and ability will be most successful. Such programmes will build on children's abilities and interests, and staff will set realistic goals for children that assist them to interact with each other. Language is one of the major tools by which adults demonstrate this to children and their parents. Language increasingly becomes one of the main tools for children's social interaction.

For children entering environments in which they do not speak the language, the development of these skills and the opportunities to practise them will be more restricted unless opportunities are provided for children to use their home languages while learning English as an additional language. In the first few months staff will need to use strategies to assist these children to enter into interactions and encourage other children to be sensitive to the needs of children learning English.

Intervention strategies can include:

- deliberately choosing children to play at activities;
- making sure the children have a staff member assigned to them so they can build strong relationships;
- using and encouraging the children's first languages;
- selecting a mix of children for stories and games;
- encouraging children who share a common first language to play together in groups;
- staff learning a few words from Amy's first language.

A programme which promotes the importance and use of all languages assists English-speaking children to value languages other than English. In these programmes, the staff could model acceptance of languages other than English, encouraging use by the children in all areas of the programme, such as spontaneous play and structured activities and games. The rest of this chapter is applicable to children from birth to 6 years.

Bilingualism

Bilingualism is a far more common phenomenon than many monolingual native speakers imagine. Over 70 per cent of the world's population speaks more than one language (Siraj-Blatchford 1994a). Thus it is as natural to grow up speaking more than one language as it is to grow up speaking only one language.

Bilingualism is the ability to understand and make oneself understood in two (or more) languages. But bilingualism can take many forms. Many bilingual people are more proficient in one of their two (or more) languages, although the language involved may not be dominant in the same contexts. For example, young bilingual children may use only English at school or in the nursery but be very proficient in their first language at home. They may find it difficult to use their home language in the early childhood setting where they might be unfamiliar with the vocabulary or context.

Young children learning English as an additional language may use both languages in the early childhood setting. This is called 'code switching'. Sometimes children change languages in the middle of a conversation or they may use words from their first language in English conversations or vice versa. Bilingual staff can help children keep the languages separate by trying to speak only one language at a time when talking to the children.

Young children have the potential to develop bilingually when they start to learn a second language from an early age. Two types of second language acquisition have been described: 'simultaneous acquisition' and 'sequential or successive acquisition'. 'Simultaneous acquisition' occurs when children are exposed to more than one language from a very early age, for example, when the father speaks one language and the mother speaks another from the time of a child's birth. 'Sequential or successive acquisition' occurs when children begin to learn a second language after the first language is partially established. For example, young children starting in the nursery or school may first acquire the home language in the family and then acquire the second or additional language when entering the early childhood setting.

Learning in two languages

If staff working with young bilingual children support the use of languages other than English, children will feel confident about using both languages. Gradually they will associate a language with a particular person or place and the two languages will be used more systematically. However, many children when they start school do not want to appear different from their English-speaking friends and may go through a stage where they are reluctant to speak the home language. Parents often report that gradually the use of English becomes dominant and children answer their parents in English. This reluctance to continue to use the home language may be affected by the attitudes shown by the community, particularly staff in the early childhood setting. Children who do not have a positive feeling about the use of their home language and who are not supported by staff may lose the ability to speak in their home language and will become 'receiving bilinguals' (able only to understand but not to speak or reply).

Often parents are concerned about the ability of the child to become bilingual, so it is important that staff, other professionals and parents have up to date information about the learning of two or more languages so that they can make informed choices. Parents and staff in early childhood settings often raise questions about bilingualism in young children. These include the following:

Should a child be exposed to two languages simultaneously or should one be established before exposure to another?

Research has shown that the first six years of life are as critical for language development as for all other development. Evidence suggests that children can easily learn more than one language from birth and in many countries this is normal language behaviour. As long as the children have plenty of opportunities to hear both languages used in normal conversations with others then they develop the ability to use more than one language. Other children may be only exposed to one language from birth but enter a new language environment when they start in the nursery. Current research indicates that it is critically important that children have the opportunity to continue developing the home language as it has been shown that a strong foundation in the first language provides the basis for later learning of the second language (Clarke 1996).

Why should we bother to bring our children up bilingually?

Research (Skutnabb-Kangas 1981; Kesslar and Quinn 1982, 1987; Hakuta 1986; Hakuta and Pease-Alvarez 1992; Milne and Clarke 1993, 1995) has shown the positive benefits of bilingualism. Some of the advantages identified in these studies are: increased self-esteem, positive identity and attitudes towards language learning, cognitive flexibility, increased problem-solving and greater metalinguistic awareness.

Isn't it too hard for young children to acquire two languages at the same time when they have so much to learn?

Research has shown that encouraging children to become bilingual can contribute to their cognitive flexibility. This means that children who are brought up bilingually learn that there is more than one way to categorize something, and more than one way to view the world (Skutnabb-Kangas 1981). The maintenance of the first language provides the opportunity to continue intellectual development while learning English. There is evidence that knowing more than one language well increases the flexibility of children's thinking (Milne and Clarke 1993).

Will maintaining the first language mean that children don't learn enough English?

For young children entering a new language environment, the continued use of the home language is important for social and personal development. The development of values and a positive sense of one's place in society is enhanced by the children's ties to larger outside groups. Within the circle of the family, the continued use of the first language is important for strengthening the bond between parents and children, and for developing the growth of trust and affection in the home.

In the early years setting there are plenty of opportunities for children to learn English as an additional language from English-speaking adults and peers. These speakers often provide better models for the children to hear English than those that might be made available at home. At the same time, the continued use of the home language in the early years environment allows children to build up their knowledge of the new environment while learning to associate English with concepts learned previously.

I want to use my language at home so my children can communicate with other family members

One of the most important reasons for continuing the use of the home language is to be able to keep links with other family members both at home and overseas, and for the maintenance of family ties and respect for elders. Parents of bilingual children often report that their children's English-speaking friends exert pressure on them as they get older, which often results in the children refusing to speak their home language and sometimes forgetting their home language entirely. Parents feel they lose control over their children.

There are economic and employment advantages in being able to communicate well in two languages. With the increasing globalization and communication many companies require staff to speak more than one language. The advantages are expected to increase with the globalization of countries, such as Australia's growing presence in Asia, and the United Kingdom's move into Europe. Given our growing recognition of global interdependence and the need to encourage greater communication and understanding, bilingualism may be seen as a major national and international asset.

The doctor (speech pathologist, neighbour, etc.) told me that my child would be at a disadvantage if I continued to speak my language at home

Unfortunately there are still a number of people in our community who confuse second language development with language delay. It is vital the early childhood staff recognize the stages children go through in learning English as an additional language and differentiate between these and the indictors of language delay. Children who are proceeding normally with the learning of English do not need to attend speech pathology sessions. Early childhood staff should reassure parents of the process of learning a new language and should work with other professionals to recognize the differences.

Maintaining the first language

In societies like the United Kingdom, the United States of America, Canada and Australia which have multilingual populations, children from linguistic minority backgrounds must learn the mainstream language in order to take full advantage of the educational opportunities available. For many children the emphasis on learning standard English has been at the expense of the home language. When language-minority children enter English-speaking classrooms they encounter powerful forces for assimilation. The children may quickly realize that their language and culture are not valued. If they want to be accepted by the majority, then there is pressure on them to speak in English, so peer, staff and community pressures quickly motivate them to speak English and to forget their home language (Wong-Fillmore 1991). The loss of the first language may have a number of consequences for the children and their families. These include:

Loss of feelings of self-worth

If children and families are unable to use their first language or if they see that their language and culture is not valued by others they see this as having no value and have doubts about themselves and their families.

Breakdown of family relationships

If children speak only English, they may lose the ability to speak the language of the home. They are then unable to communicate effectively with older family members and parents. Parents find it difficult to have conversations with their children and feel like they are losing control over their lives.

Inability of families to socialize their children into their culture

The culture and values of the family are transmitted by language. Parents are unable to pass on social ways and expectations if they do not share a common language with the children.

Loss of values, traditions, beliefs and family wisdom

If children cannot speak the language of the family, then values and cultural traditions, beliefs and family wisdom are lost.

Loss of the intimacy that comes from shared interactions between children and family members

Many parents find that the intimacy they share with their family comes from the language they know best, the language of the heart. They feel that emotions and interactions are stilted if not shared with their families in their own languages.

Loss of opportunities for continued cognitive development

If children have the opportunity to continue using the first home language in the nursery or pre-school, then the cognitive development children have begun at home can continue. Staff in early childhood settings have a vital role to play in supporting the child's continued maintenance and development of the first language. Staff need to work together with parents to encourage the children's continued first/home language development. Parents must be reassured of the benefits of bilingualism and helped to understand that the children will benefit from learning English as an additional or second language from good language models and fluent speakers of English. Staff should be aware of the harm they can do by insisting that children always speak English in the setting and at home.

Optimum time for introducing the second language

For children who have begun their development in a language other than English it is preferable that they have the opportunity to continue this development within the early childhood setting. Bilingual staff can play a crucial role in facilitating the continued use of the home language. If early childhood services do not have bilingual staff available then every effort should be made to provide and utilize bilingual resources in the programme, as well as staff supporting parents in their continued use of the first language at home.

The early years are an important time for introducing the second language. Many children entering the nursery or pre-school are already fluent in their first language. They know how language works and they know about language. They are practised at communicating with others, they just need the vocabulary and grammar in the new language to transfer knowledge and concepts from their early experiences in another language. Young learners have better chances of gaining native-like pronunciation in the second language and are more inclined to take risks with learning. Young children do not have to learn as much as adults to achieve competence in a new language. The constructions they need to use to communicate are shorter and their vocabulary is smaller.

An optimum setting for introducing a second language

Every early childhood setting has the potential to provide a natural stress-free learning environment where young children have the opportunity to practise language while trying out a range of activities. This is an ideal setting for language learning because there is so much going on that is of interest to children. Another advantage of the early childhood setting is that young children can get a great deal of meaning across using just a few single words in the second language. Children are strongly motivated to talk so as to make things happen, to make their presence felt, to contribute and to exercise some power over the world. Throughout the day children have opportunities to actively handle and explore many objects while they are learning to name them in the second language (Clarke and Milne 1996).

How does a bilingual programme or community language programme benefit other children in the early years?

A bilingual programme or a programme that offers all children the opportunity to be exposed to other languages beside English provides opportunities for all children to develop positive attitudes to other language users and other languages, and provides children with the opportunity to learn something of another language. Children in these programmes learn that English is not the only language that can be used to express ideas and actions. They learn that other languages are *different*, not 'foreign' (or 'alien' to them). In a bilingual programme which is based on the cultural and linguistic backgrounds of the children, language learning occurs naturally and all children can have fun being exposed to a wide variety of languages (Clarke and Milne 1996).

What models are best for bilingualism in the early years?

Research into bilingual early childhood programmes have shown that there are a number of ways that programmes can be organized (Milne and Clarke 1993). Early childhood settings can be adapted to provide good models of bilingual care and education. Programme models can include full bilingual programmes or programmes with some bilingual context. They may involve use of one community language and English, or several community languages and English.

Bilingual programmes should not be seen as early assimilation programmes. That is, they should not be implemented only as a transition programme until the children have learned enough English to join in with others. Rather, bilingualism should be seen as an asset and efforts should be made to continue the use of the children's home languages throughout their nursery and schooling. Efforts should be made to take advantage of the range of languages and cultures within the community. Bilingual staff need to be employed in order to facilitate the programme and so that both languages can be used throughout the day.

The preferred language policy for developing the bilingual skills of young children is the one language–one speaker model. In this model staff are employed to be designated speakers of particular languages. They use these languages most of the time with all children. Bilingual staff encourage the children to speak to them in their language rather than English. However, children may be dominant in English and prefer to speak in English, and they need to be gently encouraged to use both languages, as the following example shows:

Spanish caregiver: Este cuento se trata de un perro llamado Negro.
(*This is a story about the dog called Negro.*)
Paolo (3 years): It's a dog.
Spanish caregiver: En español se dice 'Perro'.
Paolo: 'Perro.'

The structure of the programme can take different forms: some may be highly structured or have loosely structured content, some may plan for mixed age groups, some ensuring simultaneous exposure to two or more languages throughout the day, others timetabling different language groups at different times. However the programme is organized, parents should be viewed as collaborators in their children's education and should have opportunities to be involved in the planning.

What is a bilingual programme?

A bilingual programme aims to maintain and develop the home languages of children, to introduce all children to second or additional language learning, to facilitate fluency in language development, to promote a strong self-concept with positive feelings about ethnic identity and to cultivate multicultural or pluralist perspectives (Milne and Clarke 1993: 14; Siraj-Blatchford 1994a). Bilingual programmes should be available for all children, not just those who come from language backgrounds other than English.

A bilingual programme is one in which more than one language is used throughout the day. Bilingual programmes encourage the continued use of the children's home languages and introduce English as an additional language. As suggested earlier, this continued use of the home language enables children to continue their cognitive development.

All bilingual programmes should be developmentally and culturally appropriate, and provide a range of opportunities for free play and more structured staff-initiated play. A child-centred approach, planned in consultation with parents, provides staff with opportunities to observe children and plan a programme that incorporates their cultural and socio-economic backgrounds, needs and interests. The programme should encourage the children to interact with their peers. Sometimes staff may need to structure group times to include children of the same language background.

A bilingual programme in the early years does not necessarily have to aim for equal fluency in both languages. The degree of fluency in two or more languages acquired in the early years will depend on a number of factors such as the amount of exposure to the languages, in the centre and at home. However, any exposure to a second language is an advantage as it widens young children's attitudes and ideas about language.

The following are practical strategies for making early childhood settings bilingual:

- actively recruit and employ bilingual staff;
- ensure that all written materials for parents are in the home languages and English;
- make sure the physical environment reflects the home languages and cultures of the children;
- select books and puzzles which portray the diversity of the society in a

positive way and which represent languages other than English as well as English;
- encourage staff to use the one language–one speaker model;
- use each of the languages at routine times as well as encouraging use when children play inside and outside;
- ensure bilingual staff use their first/home languages as much as possible;
- assist bilingual staff to add to the bilingual resources available;
- plan group times in both languages every day;
- make sure rooms contain examples of the print of languages used by the children.

Working with bilingual staff

A major factor in supporting young bilingual children in the early years is the employment of bilingual staff to work in all areas of the programme. Bilingual staff play a vital role in the programme and need to be supported in the work they do with children and families. The following strategies have been found useful:

Bilingual staff need to plan for regular opportunities to work with children in their home language

- to meet the child on arrival to help settle the child in to activities;
- to explain the activities and routines in the child's own language;
- to encourage learners to use their home language;
- to introduce children to others who speak the same language;
- to extend the learner's first language through stories, songs and games;
- to take regular groups in the home languages;
- to assist children to understand changes in routine;
- to plan activities which assist children to interact with others.

Bilingual staff need to provide a good language model for the children

- do not mix the languages when speaking with children;
- do not correct children's mistakes but model and expand the language;
- use a variety of resources to extend children's learning in their own language.

Bilingual staff have a vital role in working with other staff in the programme

- meet regularly with other staff to discuss the progress children are making in their first and second language;
- assist staff to understand the cultural backgrounds of children;
- communicate the wishes of parents to the staff;
- contribute to individual records of the child;
- report on the progress of a child to other staff and to parents;
- contribute to the development of centre policy;
- contribute to staff meetings and planning times;
- contribute to parent newsletters.

Bilingual staff can assist parents to understand the programmes and philosophies of the nursery or school

- meet parents on arrival to explain the programme;
- interpret between staff and parents;
- assist with home visits;
- explain the policy of the centre;
- answer parents' concerns;
- participate in enrolment days.

(Clarke 1999)

Fahzal is 3½ years old. He was born in Iran but his family has been in Bradford for two years. He lives with his mother, father and grandmother. Farsi is the only language spoken at home.

Fahzal began nursery at 3 years of age. He had no previous contact with other children or exposure to English. From the first few days he was very unhappy, he cried on arrival for the first week and was reluctant to leave his mother. She was also upset and embarrassed by his clinging behaviour. The mother was encouraged to stay with him for a few days.

After several weeks, Fahzal was still very reticent to join in but was happy to come to the nursery. He would settle at table activities if directed by the teacher but did not spontaneously choose to play. He refused to speak in Farsi or to attempt any English. After two months attendance, the teacher was concerned that Fahzal refused to join in English groups and would not speak any English.

Fahzal was the only Farsi speaker in the nursery, although there were other Farsi-speaking children in the school. A Farsi-speaking bilingual support teacher was available in the school but had not made contact with Fahzal.

The case study opposite illustrates practical strategies for supporting young bilingual children as they settle into nursery or school.

- What are the issues highlighted in the case study?
- What further information do you need?
- What strategies could you implement in your programme?

Even if there are no bilingual children in your setting this is an interesting case study to discuss, every setting now has the potential to enrol a child with a similar background to that of Fahzal.

Staff checklist

Use the following checklist with your staff to see if you are meeting the needs of the bilingual children in your centre.

Indicator	Yes	No	Need to work on this
The centre/school has a written policy about the centre in community languages as well as English			
Staff are knowledgeable about the children's cultural background			
Staff make efforts to accommodate parents' views			
Bilingual parents are informed in their own language about the programme			
The environment reflects the cultural/linguistic/socio/economic/gender backgrounds of all the children			
There are bilingual notices displayed			
Bilingual staff are employed in the programme			
Bilingual staff are encouraged to use their first languages with the children at all times			
Bilingual staff are involved in programme planning			
Bilingual staff are encouraged to teach all children songs, words and greetings from their first languages			
Bilingual staff are encouraged to develop resources in the first language (books, board games, song cards, story tapes, wall displays)			

Indicator	Yes	No	Need to work on this
There are regular group times in languages other than English			
The children are actively encouraged to speak in their first/home languages			
The children are grouped together with others who speak the same language			
There is a library of bilingual books for children to borrow			
Bilingual staff/interpreters are always available for enrolment sessions and parent meetings			
English speaking staff try to learn something of the children's first languages			

This chapter has addressed the value of bilingualism and supporting bilingual children in their development. The importance of acknowledging the social and cultural influences of the children's background has been highlighted. It has been shown that bilingualism is a positive benefit to all for educational, social, economic and family reasons. The knowledge and skills that young bilingual learners bring to the early childhood setting is supported by staff who understand that learners come from linguistically and culturally diverse settings. Staff need to acknowledge the valuable contribution made to the children's development by the family and recognize that oral and literacy traditions vary across cultures. This is a vital part of maintaining and sustaining children's positive self-esteem and identity, and ensuring that they feel secure and an emotional sense of well-being. In Chapter 3, children's second language acquisition will be discussed further and strategies given for assisting children in early years settings.

Further reading

Clarke, P.M. (1992) *English as a 2nd Language in Early Childhood*. Victoria, Australia: Free Kindergarten Association.

Gonzales-Mena, J. (1998) *Foundations: Early Childhood Education in a Diverse Society*. Mountain View, CA: Mayfield Publishing.

Milne, R. and Clarke, P. (1993) *Bilingual Early Childhood Education in Child Care and Preschool Centres*. Victoria, Australia: FKA Multicultural Resource Centre.

Tabors, P.O. (1997) *One Child, Two Languages; A Guide for Preschool Educators of Children Learning English as a Second Language.* Baltimore, MD: Paul Brookes Publishing Co.

Trevarthen, C. (1992) An infant's motives for thinking and speaking in the culture, in A.H. Wold (ed.) *The Dialogical Alternative*, pp. 99–137. Oxford: Oxford University Press.

3

Learning English as an additional language

Figure 3.1 Young children need to communicate with each other as well as with adults in their home language
Photograph: Sally Abbott Smith

First and second language development in babies and toddlers

In an ideal child care setting, babies and toddlers would hear their own language for most of the time. However, this is not always possible. As this is a crucial time for developing language, staff, parents and carers need to provide support for young learners through direct, personal communication.

During the first 12 months, the most important thing for babies are voices and faces to listen to and focus on. Staff need to remember to speak directly with the babies so they can watch the movement of their lips. The following are important strategies for helping babies and toddlers develop language:

- make sure the babies and toddlers can see your face when you talk to them;
- listen and respond to their language play;
- play turn-taking games;
- sing and coo to babies, encourage sound play and babbling;
- show pictures and objects when you talk so a baby can identify objects with words and use labelling techniques;
- use plenty of repetition and imitation;
- provide good language models;
- keep the conversations simple;
- encourage toddlers to say words;
- copy the words and sounds made by toddlers;
- give babies and toddlers board books and magazines to look at;
- read stories every day;
- make sure you have plenty of physical contact;
- have lots of fun;
- use short sentences and speak clearly;
- involve bilingual adults and parents as much as possible;
- encourage bilingual parents to speak their home language as much as possible;
- learn words, rhymes and songs in other languages.

It is essential to remember that communication is a two-way process, and speech is made up of a series of turns. When adults talk with children, they should provide opportunities for children to talk to them. Pauses must be left in conversations. Questions need to be simple. Children need language for developing thinking, and the more thinking they are doing the more their language will develop. At this stage, there is no need to correct pronunciation or grammar. Staff should model and expand the language used by the children (Siraj-Blatchford 1994a; Clarke 1996).

The following strategies are useful for developing language in 2- to 3-year-olds:

- read and tell stories every day;
- develop conversations about activities;
- plan group times to involve three or four children;
- expand and model conversations;
- teach simple songs and rhymes;
- learn rhymes and songs in other languages;
- encourage the continued use of the home language;
- teach lots of repetitive rhymes and games;
- support conversations with visual materials;
- make sure children have fun using language.

Second language acquisition in 3–6-year-olds

Unlike first language development which occurs from birth, second language acquisition can occur at any time. Research suggests that the following interrelated elements make a difference to the way children approach the learning of a second language and their ability to interact with others (Clarke 1996; Tabors 1997).

- some children are more outgoing and are risk takers;
- some children have more ability as second language learners;
- some children are more motivated to learn the second language;
- the way the environment is set up and the availability of scaffolds to assist learners can enhance or inhibit learning.

Two different portraits of the second language acquisition of young children in nursery settings follow. The characteristics of their learning are described. It will be seen that this learning is influenced by the children's personalities and willingness to use English, and that both children progress through stages of second language development.

Two case studies

> **Imran – boy, 4 years old on entry to nursery**
>
> *The nursery environment*
> - There was a bilingual programme – staff who spoke the children's first languages;
> - the programme was developmentally appropriate;
> - children's individual needs were catered for.

Characteristics of the learner
- could speak only Panjabi;
- was outgoing in his personality;
- wanted to make friends with others;
- was willing to use English immediately;
- was confident in his choice of activities;
- was eager to interact with the teacher.

Imran – English language learning
- tried to use English from his first days in the nursery;
- made friends with English speakers;
- used mainly single words;
- called out and attracted the teacher's attention;
- used a lot of repetition;
- eventually could speak in sentences.

When Imran was building with Raymond he used the few words he knew to attract Raymond's attention:

Imran (4 years 6 months): Look, look me,
Raymond (4 years): Ooh a gun, big gun, you can make me a big one, a big gun like that,
Imran: Look, look,
Raymond: You make a gun for one? ok?
Imran: Yeh. . . like this, you see? this, . . .
Raymond: Can I have that?
Imran: Yeh,
Raymond: You make one for Leroy? one, you one?
Imran: Yeh, hey look, look, look at me, look.

The staff
- responded to Imran's demands;
- supported the use of the children's first language;
- provided a rich language environment;
- offered a programme which provided a balance between structured and unstructured activities;
- provided group times every day – large and small.

The description of Imran provides us with a picture of a young boy keen to interact with others and to attempt English although his vocabulary was limited. Imran's desire to be accepted by other children and his outgoing personality ensured that he continued to develop his English.

Meena – girl, 4 years old on entry to nursery

Characteristics of the learner
- could only speak Hindi;
- was initially shy and did not want to play with others;
- took a long time to become familiar with the new environment;
- did not make any special friends;
- did not seek the teacher's attention;
- spoke mainly in home language for the first six months;
- loved music times.

The nursery environment
- had a bilingual programme which supported Meena in her use of Hindi at first;
- the programme was developmentally appropriate;
- catered for individual needs;
- the unstructured programme allowed Meena to settle in gradually without pressures;
- daily music groups provided a way into English for Meena.

Meena – English language learning
- did not use English in the first few months;
- learned English initially through singing;
- used mainly single words;
- seldom tried to attract the staff's attention;
- eventually used a lot of repetition;
- eventually could speak in sentences.

The staff
- recognized that Meena needed time to settle in;
- supported the use of the child's first language;
- did not force Meena to use English;
- introduced Meena to other children through small group activities.

The bilingual nursery environment, and the use of Panjabi and Hindi by other children and staff, provided a secure route for Meena, using her Hindi, into social interactions. Meena was able to learn the routines of the nursery and join in interactions, first using non-verbal language and her mother tongue. Meena gradually started to use English, restricted mainly to responses, particularly single words like 'yes' and 'no'.

These case studies provide individual descriptions of two young children's initiations into English as an additional language. It can be seen that the personalities of the children and their levels of motivation affected their means of entry into the English language. However, the bilingual environment and the supportive way the adults worked with the children enabled them to develop English, first single words and formulaic language and then short sentences and more complex grammar. From the descriptions it can be seen that an outgoing confident child like Imran can achieve social competence with minimal use of English. In contrast, a shy child like Meena, initially unwilling to take risks in a new language was more reluctant to enter into social interaction without the support of the teacher or a more confident child.

Children learning English as an additional language are in danger of being isolated by other children or staff. They may be ignored by English-speaking children who find it difficult to communicate with them. The environment may be unfamiliar and there may not be opportunities for the learners to hear and continue to use their home languages. Second language learners may spend their time alone, they may wait for other children to initiate conversations or they may rely on the adults to draw them into interactions. However, it is possible to assist children to enter into interactions and facilitate their progress in the second language.

Although there are individual differences in the way children acquire a second language, there are consistent phases of second language acquisition.

1 continued use of the home language in the new language context;
2 use of non-verbal communication;
3 a period of silence;
4 use of repetition and language play;
5 use of single words, formulae and routines;
6 development of more complex English.

(Clarke 1996)

1 Continued use of the home language

When young children from language backgrounds other than English enter a new predominantly English-speaking environment they may decide to continue using their home language as a means of communication. Initially this may be their only option if they have not experienced English previously. Depending on the willingness of staff and other children to accept the use of this language or depending on whether there are opportunities for children to hear and use languages other than English, children may choose to use the home language. If these children receive messages that this use of languages other than English is not acceptable, then children may revert to silence.

In a bilingual pre-school in an inner Melbourne area, learners new to English felt comfortable in their choice to continue speaking their home language while beginning to speak in English. The following strategies were used to ensure that children could maintain their first language, have their cultural background acknowledged and were provided with opportunities to learn English:

- bilingual staff were employed;
- the staff used the one language–one speaker model;
- regular group times were held in the home languages of the children and in English;
- during activities and at routine times staff spoke to the children in their own language and in English;
- the environment reflected the children's culture and language;
- all the children learned songs and games in languages other than English;
- books and games were available in languages other than English and in English;
- festivals and important milestones in children's lives were celebrated.

(Clarke 1996)

The bilingual programme supported the children's development across all areas. The staff in this nursery setting supported the children's use of the home language. They were never heard to direct the children in which language to use. The children showed that their bilingualism was a resource across the varied settings of the centre as well as within their family. For example, the children could play with peers who spoke the same language or they could play with English-speaking peers. They could communicate their needs easily in their home language at a time when their use of English was much more restricted. They could express their fears and emotions in the language they were familiar with.

2 Use of non-verbal communication

When young children are exposed to a language environment in which they do not know the language, they may be reluctant to attempt to speak in English. However, they do not necessarily stop communicating but use non-verbal means, including nodding or shaking their heads, pointing and touching and maintenance of eye contact. The physical tactics used by children when they first start in the nursery include eye contact, use of facial expressions, hand movements and tugging clothes. Non-verbal communication makes it possible for children to communicate long before they can use the appropriate verbal forms. For non-verbal behaviours to be successful, adults need to interpret the messages the learner is trying to send and should also be willing to follow through on the learners' requests.

This non-verbal behaviour can also be observed in English-speaking children if they are shy or reluctant to interact on entry to nursery or school. The same strategies used to support English as an additional language can be used with all children.

3 A period of silence

Exposure to a new language in a strange environment may result in some children entering a period of time when they do not talk at all. This period of time is often referred to as 'the silent period'. It is important for staff to understand that remaining silent is normal behaviour for some children when they start to learn a second language. This period can last for a few weeks or it can last for months.

What is happening to the children's learning at this time? Are they just listening but not learning or is this a time when learning is taking place? Studies of young children learning a second language have shown that children are absorbing the new language at this time and are building up their comprehension (Clarke 1996). Some children will communicate non-verbally during a silent period and may speak a few words such as 'yes' and 'no'. They do not withdraw completely from interaction but staff need to be aware of these children and help them to be included in interactions. Features of the silent period may include all or some of the following:

- refusal to interact in any way or be included in interactions;
- initially no use of non-verbal behaviours;
- reluctance to respond with gestures or eye contact;
- rejection of interaction with other children or staff;
- reluctance to speak (may also be in first language);
- difficulties in settling into the nursery or school.

Children in a silent period often appear to be unwilling to interact. Staff must try to make the children feel comfortable in activities with other children. Staff can help them by introducing them into small groups and by encouraging other children to include them in their play. As they often do not seek out interactions or call out to attract attention like other children, they are in danger of becoming isolated from the main opportunities for English interaction.

Strategy adopted by adults working with a child in a 'silent period'

Raj was a 4-year-old Hindi-speaking boy who started at a nursery without any previous exposure to English. Initially he was very shy. He preferred to play with quiet activities such as puzzles and blocks, where he could play alone without having to interact with other children. However, he did not refuse to do any of the tasks that adults offered to him. This solitary play continued for several months. During these initial months, the teacher encouraged him to take part in Hindi language groups with the Hindi bilingual co-worker. The teacher also continued to speak to him in English and set up opportunities for Raj to play alongside other children.

In the first weeks, Raj made few attempts to play with other children or engage them in conversations, either in Hindi or English. The teacher did not force him to join in groups if he did not wish to participate. After several months he gradually showed more confidence in choosing his own activities. By this time the teacher was gently encouraging him to join in non-verbally. After seven months in the nursery Raj began to attach himself occasionally to a group of Hindi-speaking boys and follow them around. At the same time, Raj also developed a friendship with a Chinese-speaking boy, William. This friendship, which was encouraged by the staff, played a major part in Raj's use of English. The teacher set up group times for them and encouraged their limited use of English by praising their minimal efforts.

In the final week that Raj attended the nursery, he was observed to have an extensive and sustained conversation in English with William. In this conversation he used both single words and short sentences.

For staff working with children a number of strategies can be used to support children in a silent period:

- opportunities for the children to continue learning and using the first language;
- no pressure on the children to have to speak either in English or in their first language;
- gentle assistance to the children to understand the routines and activities of the nursery or school;
- bilingual support for the children including instructions in both the first language and English;
- continued inclusion of the children in group times;
- continued conversations in English with the children even if they do not respond;

- acceptance and praise of the minimal efforts m̲a̲
  act, including acceptance of non-verbal respons
- assistance in establishing friendships with other

4 Repetition and language play

Repetition is an important strategy in the early phas
acquisition, both as a way to practise the new lan
strategy (Clarke 1996; Tabors 1997). Through their ι ̲ ̲ ̲.̲ ̲ ̲ ̲ ̲ ̲ ̲.̲.̲ ̲ ̲ ̲ ̲ ̲ ̲ ̲ ̲, children acquire a repertoire of social formulae which can be used to facilitate
interaction with others. Young children use repetition to attract attention
and to indicate to their listeners that they are willing to respond in some
way and be part of English interactions. The use of repetition provides a
way for young learners to respond immediately and can be used by learners to answer questions and to learn new vocabulary.

While the teacher was reading a story to the children, Layla used repetition to gain her attention by repeating the same word, by making noises
and by mimicking the last words of other children's phrases.

> *Teacher:* You have a look, it's a rabbit
> *Layla (3 years 6 months):* A rabbit
> *Annie:* A rabbit, see
> *Layla:* A rabbit, a rabbit
> *Teacher:* How many rabbits are there Layla? How many can you see?
> *Layla:* How many, how many

5 The use of formulae, routines and single words

In the nursery, children are exposed to a range of phrases and expressions
associated with activities such as greeting the children on arrival, the routine language used at 'mat times' and in singing. Staff also use routine
language including invitations to play, commands, turn-taking routines
and warnings and can express approval of learners' efforts including
'well done', 'good shot'.

The use of these routine phrases, sometimes called 'chunked language'
or 'formulae', is an important feature of second language acquisition as
it can assist learners to develop self-confidence and interact with others.
Routines and formulae are units of language that the learners remember
as a single prefabricated item. They are used repeatedly in routine situations as part of everyday social interaction. When learners use these
ready made phrases they show other children that they are trying to enter
into conversations with them. The formulae and chunks of languages used

by second language learners are often more grammatically ...ced in structure than other language used at the time. They can ...lude memorized sequences such as in singing and counting, swear words, exclamations, greetings, social control phrases, expressions of approval or disapproval, checks for confirmation and small talk.

An example of a chunk of language used by a young learner of English was the formulaic use of a routine phrase 'happy birthday'. This is a phrase commonly heard in nursery as children often share their birthdays with other children and sometimes bring a cake from home. It is also not uncommon to see the children making 'birthday cakes' in their play in the sandpit. The following example took place in an inner urban pre-school in Melbourne, Australia:

> Khoa learned the routine attached to 'happy birthday' and much of her play for the entire year in the sand pit revolved around this activity. The phrases 'happy birthday' and 'happy birthday to you' were used by her in her play. She used the phrase 'happy birthday to you' to mean a cake, when she said; 'I'm making a happy birthday to you, at other times she just used the phrase 'happy birthday'. For example, 'this is a happy birthday'.

> (Clarke 1996)

Staff can also use routine language in a variety of settings to cue learners. Once the learners have become absorbed in the context of the group, they learn social cues that help them to make sense of the actions of other children and copy them. This can show the staff that the learner knows what is going on. Amira loved singing times and gained confidence in participating. She used the routine phrases she acquired to build a repertoire of English and to assist her to take part in interactions. In the following example, a word used by the teacher triggered the singing of a song Amira had already learned. One day Amira was playing with a puzzle. The teacher was sitting beside her and looked at the picture of the fruit in the puzzle. She asked Amira (4 years), 'Where are the bananas?' Amira started to sing 'bananas in pyjamas are coming down the stairs', the teacher joined in with her and Amira sang the song.

Another example of routines commonly used are 'interactive rhymes' (Ratner and Bruner 1978; Bruner and Sherwood 1981). These rhymes are commonly used in social exchanges between adults and young children and involve predictable words and actions. For example, the exchange between a parent and child – What does the doggie say? Child: 'woof woof'. These early interactions often provide the first systematic uses of language with an adult at first playing both parts, answering and acting for the child, but including the child in as much action as possible. As the

child gradually learns the sequence, the adult sh[...]
child's participation and praises the child for appr[...]

Interactive rhymes are fun things to do with a[...] ticularly helpful for encouraging young children l[...] combine the elements of having fun with languag[...] and learning to take turns. At first, children can rely[...] guage which makes up the predictable responses. T[...] whether verbal or non-verbal, can be responded to i[...] adults who can expand the utterances.

Books and storytime provide many opportunities for developing these interactive patterns. Consider the following example in which the teacher is reading the story *The Very Hungry Caterpillar* (Carle 1969) to a small group of children. This story makes extensive use of repetitive sentences, providing opportunities for word substitution.

> *Adult:* On Monday he ate one apple, but he was still hungry. On Tues-
> day he ate two . . .
> *Ali (4 years):* Pears but he was still hungry
> *Adult:* On Wednesday . . .
> *Ali:* He ate three – we could say three 'Big Mac'
> *Adult:* That's a good idea, we could make up our own food couldn't
> we?

The teacher uses the moment to encourage the child's own attempts at interacting, by encouraging Ali's spontaneous attempts to join in and to contribute his own ideas.

Young learners also rely heavily on the use of single words in the initial stages of second language acquisition. At this time, much of the language used concerns the identification and naming of objects in the classroom. Initially when asked 'what's this?' children reply with the name of an object. If they do not know, the staff usually supplies the answer and the learner repeats the name. As the learner's confidence grows, it is usual for them to volunteer the names of the objects often before the question is asked.

The first vocabulary of single words used includes names and labels, action words. The use of high utility phrases, such as 'yes', 'no', 'bye-bye', 'excuse me', 'hey', 'OK' and 'I don't know' are commonly used by second language learners in the early years. This use of single words, particularly calls, assists learners to gain entry and to sustain their participation in interactions.

complex English

e children have begun to acquire a vocabulary of useful items and hrases they can build on this, extending the single words and chunks of language into more complex uses of language. Once this stage of development is reached, children begin to put together longer more complex sentences which express limited but relevant meaning. Sometimes the children will combine some of the chunks they have acquired.

During water play, Rani holds the bucket up to the teacher:

Rani (4 years): I want here, more, I want here more, more, more, more.
Adult: Do you want to do more?
Rani: I want to. She picks up a watering can.
Adult: Come on and I'll get you some water.
Rani: I want put here, want it here (*Rani points into the watering can*).

Young learners can generate sentences by combining routine phrases such as 'I want', 'look at . . .' with nouns, pronouns and adjectives. In other situations, learners will combine their use of single words with short sentences containing verbs. As learners gain confidence, they can use more elaborated noun phrases, for example adding the definite and indefinite article. As children begin to construct sentences in meaningful ways, they pay attention to the way elements are changed as the meaning changes, for example, changing singular to plural, present to past tense or by changing verb endings.

During the children's early experimentation with more complex uses of language, mistakes commonly occur in the learners' English use. This can be seen when children are moving away from more formulaic uses of language. It is important not to correct children when they make mistakes but model the correct constructions in sentences, encouraging the learners to continue the conversation. In the following example, you can see the way the teacher assisted Mehmet without discouraging his attempts at talking. Mehmet and his teacher were looking at photos Mehmet had brought from home:

Teacher: Did you have a picnic?
Mehmet (3 years 9 months): A picnic. Yes. Over there. (*He points to the next photo*)
Teacher: Oh I can see you sitting at the bench having a picnic lunch. Did you have sandwiches?
Mehmet: No sandwiches. I meat. Barbecue.
Teacher: Oh a barbecue with meat. Did your dad make that?
Mehmet: No Dad, me and Khan.
Teacher: Oh not your dad, you and your brother Khan.

As this example shows, the teacher kept Mehmet engaged in the conversation, continually expanding his limited English and modelling the correct constructions. This ensured that Mehmet was engaged in the function of the interaction and he did not need to worry about getting the grammar right.

Young learners learn the functions of negation very early. However, it takes some time before they learn the grammar rules which enable them to express the variety of negative functions. These functions provide opportunities for children to deny, reject, refuse something and disagree with others. Initially, young children use 'no' and 'not' and formulae such as 'I can't' and 'don't'. As they develop more complex language they begin to combine the negative with other words as the following example shows. Kassia is sitting with the teacher doing a puzzle together. Another child, Boris comes over and shows the teacher a chocolate he has:

Teacher: Is that your chocolate?
Boris (3 years 6 months):   Chocolate.
Kassia (3 years 6 months): I have no chocolate. (*Kassia reaches for the chocolate*)
Boris: No. Don't.

At the same time that children are developing more complex structures in their use of negatives, they are also beginning to use more complex forms of questions. There is a remarkable consistency in the way children learn to form questions in English. Initially the first question forms used by young learners are inflected single words and the use of single 'wh' words. First, 'what', 'where' and 'who' are used, then 'when' and 'how' (Lightbown and Spada 1995: 61). Ramese is doing a cat puzzle, he holds up a piece of puzzle and calls out to the teacher, but she is not listening to him:

Ramese (4 years): Judy, this where? this where? this where Judy?
Ramese: Judy, this where? Judy, where?
Teacher: Will I show you where to put it?

In the early stages of learning English, young children may use only single word questions. As staff are able to build on what the children say, this use of words such as 'what', 'where' and 'why' is initially enough for the learners to take part in conversations. The above example shows that the children's capacity to communicate in the early phases is well in advance of their ability to use complex English structures.

In summary, it can be seen that children learning English as an additional language go through a number of stages. In the next part of this chapter, the role of the context, including the role of the staff in setting up and interacting with children will be discussed. A major factor in children's successful acquisition of the second language is the provision of a rich environment which will support children's efforts at learning. The learners' attitudes to learning and their confidence in themselves are key factors.

Principles of supporting bilingual children

As previously suggested, all children in the early years benefit from a rich language environment and programmes that focus on learners new to English are equally valuable for all children. Research has shown that staff have a major role in supporting learners, this includes encouraging the learners to start to use English, supporting and scaffolding their interaction and extending and building on their use of English (Clarke 1996; Tabors 1997).

The task of learning English as an additional language is a long-term one. Learners who are new to English need a planned programme over a sustained period of time in order to succeed in the mainstream curriculum of the early years. Any English as an additional language programme for young children must be based on sound principles for language teaching and learning. The following principles apply specifically to children in the years prior to school entry and have been adapted by Clarke (1997) from eight principles of language teaching and learning for school aged children included in the McKay and Scarino (1991: 28–30) *ESL Framework of Stages*. Strategies for implementing these principles are also given.

Principle 1

Young children learning English as an additional language should be treated as individuals with their own needs and interests. Staff / Adults need to:

- work closely with parents and other significant caregivers to find out the needs and interests of individual children;
- plan for all the children's interests in a range of areas – physical, social, emotional, intellectual, linguistic and cultural;
- develop a sense of trust to encourage children to take risks in language use;
- provide time for children to get used to the new environment;
- recognize that children may not want to speak immediately;

- plan a variety of groups and use different teaching strategies, such as team teaching;
- provide opportunities for pair work and small group work to assist in the development of social skills.

Principle 2

Young children learning English as an additional language should be encouraged to participate in a wide range of activities which encourage communication. Staff need to:

- provide a range of predictable, routine activities;
- provide opportunities for spontaneous play;
- encourage children who speak the same first language to play together and use their first language;
- provide a mix of structured and unstructured groups;
- provide opportunities for children to hear and practise the same language (in context) in many different ways;
- include children in regular activities rather than withdrawing them from the mainstream;
- provide a variety of activities using a range of appropriately graded materials which reflect the children's language ability and comprehension.

Principle 3

Young children learning English as an additional language should have access to an environment that reflects their own cultural and linguistic backgrounds. Staff need to:

- find out information about the cultural and linguistic backgrounds of the children in the group;
- plan a programme which reflects the diversity of the group;
- create an environment where the children feel comfortable and want to join in;
- design activities based on familiar experiences and cultural events;
- show young learners that the centre values the first language spoken by them and their families;
- encourage children to continue to use their home language.

Principle 4

Young children learning English as an additional language should be exposed to language they can understand and which is appropriate to their level of development. Staff need to:

- create an atmosphere which encourages children to interact in English;
- accept and positively acknowledge all attempts to communicate, whether verbal or non-verbal;
- use easy to understand directions, repeat and model language, and monitor the way children are spoken to by adults;
- introduce new vocabulary gradually, use simple grammatical structures and few idioms;
- support talk with clear visuals, such as pictures, photos and toys;
- allow time for children to process information and to decide on an appropriate response;
- look for signs of understanding such as willingness to listen, willingness to participate; appropriate responses to context such as laughing at stories, joining in actions in songs and games.

Principle 5

Young children learning English as an additional language should be exposed to language that is meaningful, based on their concrete experiences and supported by visual materials. Staff need to:

- plan activities based on familiar experiences and build on prior knowledge when introducing new language items;
- support conversations with materials such as pictures, photos, toys, games, picture lotto and books;
- plan activities in which children have plenty of opportunities to handle materials;
- keep activities short but allow time within the group for children to process new information;
- learn to identify signs of growing comprehension as well as identify signs of confusion or loss of interest.

Principle 6

Young children learning English as an additional language should participate in frequent interactions with adults and children. Staff need to:

- provide a variety of group times which involve an adult and other children;
- use a variety of techniques which encourage the learner to speak English, such as modelling and extending language and building on the language used by the children even if very minimal;
- plan interactive situations which encourage dialogue between the learner, other children and adults;

- encourage the learners to build relationships with other children;
- provide group times for children together who speak the same first language.

Principle 7

Young children learning English as an additional language should be encouraged and praised and receive appropriate support and feedback from adults. Staff need to:

- accept the children's minimal efforts, including non-verbal responses;
- praise children's efforts, using a range of routine expressions such as 'good shot', 'well done', 'good work', 'great'.
- provide regular feedback;
- set realistic and achievable goals so children can experience success and to promote self-esteem.

Principle 8

Young children learning English as an additional language should be in an environment where the focus is on the meaning and not on the form (words and grammar). Staff need to:

- practise pronunciation in fun ways;
- allow time for children to practise informally as well as on more formal occasions;
- use speech rhymes, songs and chants to develop rhythm and fluency;
- use intonation to highlight patterns in shared-book readings, rhymes and songs;
- encourage the children to make up their own chants or complete chants or lines in stories;
- use music, rhythm, pitch and clapping activities to show stress, loudness, softness and tone;
- correct children's errors by repeating sentences in the correct form or modelling correct language in another way.

Supporting learners in the early days of nursery and school

In the early days of nursery and school, the difference between receptive language (what children understand) and expressive language (what they can say) is quite marked in young children learning English as an additional language. Initially, even though children may show through other means that they understand what is being said to them, they may use English only in singing, counting or with formulaic responses. Clarke (1999) suggests the following strategies for supporting children in their early years:

Use of predictable routines and behavioural expectations

In the early months of the year in the nursery and school, staff need to work persistently to establish predictable routines and behavioural expectations for the learners. These include greeting the children on arrival, and making use of routine language each day to assist children to choose from a range of activities, for example, invitations to play – 'What would you like to do today?', 'Come and sit down here'. Staff can model language patterns in routine classroom language for example, 'Today is . . .', 'Yesterday was . . .'. Other routine language can be used to assist children with changes in activities and group times, such as: 'Come and sit on the mat'; 'Are you all watching?'; 'Ready?'; 'Stand up'; 'Sit down'. Staff can use a variety of language games for dispersal to activities.

Use of positive feedback

The children's level of confidence will affect the degree to which they are willing to take risks in the use of English. A child who is confident to try new vocabulary or to take part in conversations will appear to be more competent with language than a child who is shy or worries about making mistakes. These children may remain silent for some time in a new language environment. Children need to be given positive, encouraging feedback in any attempts they make to communicate in English. This includes their non-verbal responses. Feedback can include generous use of praise such as 'good shot', 'well done', 'great'.

Developing listening skills

Listening is an integral part of any early years programme and for young English as an additional language learners, learning to listen is critical. In order to interact children need to listen to what is being said, to interpret the speaker's meaning, to formulate an answer and respond (Jalongo 1996: 21).

The tasks that young children have to deal with while learning English as an additional language are many and children also have to develop complex understandings in order to use the new language. They have to learn:

- to recognize new non-verbal language, gestures and facial expressions;
- to distinguish sounds;
- to understand new vocabulary;
- to identify individual words from what initially sounds like a continuous string of sounds;
- to recognize a new script or alphabet;
- to recognize differences in stress, rhythm and intonation;
- to differentiate the structure of the new language (including word order, use of definite and indefinite articles, etc.);
- to adopt new ways of behaving and new values;
- to understand jokes, metaphors and idiomatic language.

(adapted from ESL Essentials. Directorate of School Education 1992: 17)

Because of the complex nature of learning an additional language, young learners may take some time to tune in and listen actively to the sounds of English. Staff must assist children to develop listening skills. The following strategies can be used by staff to model good listening skills and encourage children to listen actively:

- model good listening habits by getting down to the child's eye level;
- concentrate on what the child is saying – knowing when to listen and when to talk;
- create a positive listening environment where background sounds or music is eliminated so that children can focus on listening;
- ensure that all children can be heard – this may mean explaining to others that everyone needs to have a turn. Check that the learner has understood what you said;
- plan listening activities and games based on the children's level of development, interests and experiences and supported with real objects and pictures, for example, music, singing games, audio tapes and sound and picture recognition);
- use strategies to increase active listening, such as restating ('Who can tell me what we need to do before we do a painting?'), summarizing ('What did we do when we went on the excursion?'), reflecting ('If you could . . .') and self assessment ('Tell us . . .');
- read and tell a wide variety of stories and involve the children as much as possible in patterned responses. Support stories with props and visual materials;
- encourage the children to dramatize the story or illustrate the story with puppets.

Practising pronunciation

Children learning English as an additional language need many opportunities to listen to and practise English before they are familiar with the pronunciation, sounds, stress and rhythms of the new language. They need a variety of activities that provide practice of the new sounds and plenty of encouragement to become proficient. Depending on their age when they begin to learn the new language, children may continue to speak with an accent. However, introducing sounds and rhymes in fun ways will give children practice in the new language. Strategies for teaching and support include:

- providing opportunities for children to hear language sounds and patterns modelled by native speakers;
- using speech rhymes, clapping activities, songs and chants to develop fluency and rhythm;
- encouraging children to fill in repetitive choruses in stories and rhymes;
- using tongue twisters and funny rhymes.

Use of contextualized language

In the early years, most of the learning focuses on the 'here and now'. Staff can build on this by focusing on topics and activities that build on common experiences and that can provide shared background knowledge for children. Staff need to extend learning opportunities by planning activities that provide opportunities for the children to identify meaning through the context. Use of 'hands on' activities, support from visual materials and other activities which focus on personal and concrete experiences support learners to develop important concepts and learn key language items in English. As their knowledge of English improves they gradually construct more meaning from the words themselves but the construction is often incomplete.

Use of concrete referents

Another important scaffold to support young learners in the early years is the use of concrete referents, such as non-verbal cues, gestures and visual aids to support the language learning. The content of language directed at learners should enable the learners to identify the meaning through the immediate context (Dulay, Burt and Krashen 1982). Visual, contextual and linguistic cues are important as they make it possible for learners to enter interactions. Linguistic cues include calls to attract and hold attention, repetition and cues to identify objects.

Another important aspect is the use of familiar topics to assist learners. If learners are able to enter into interactions using language and experiences that are familiar this gives them confidence.

Use of decontextualized language

Young learners gain confidence with their use of English and become less reliant on concrete referents. As they develop confidence in the use of English, it is important to expose them to more 'decontextualized language', that is, the language of 'there and then', which is often the language of stories, of recounting events that happened at some other time and of reference texts that will be used in learning. Children need opportunities in interaction to indicate their interests, opinions and preferences and to learn to negotiate solutions to problems, interpersonal situations and conflict.

With fluency in the second or additional language children's comprehension increases and they are able to use more complex constructions. Staff have a major role in supporting both the learners' acquisition of comprehension and their production of English. Staff need to build on the learners' attempts at conversation, use the context to provide the learner with clues to the conversation, model and expand the correct form and avoid using idiomatic language. During conversations, adults can help the learners by prompting them and filling in gaps in the conversations.

Early childhood educators and parents often regard language as the central vehicle through which children learn and make sense of their cultural environment. Language is also deeply rooted in culture and therefore a vital component of how we feel about ourselves. Children need a good image of themselves, and valuing and extending their linguistic competencies and awareness is vital to this process. Self-esteem and identity are based largely on competent acquisition of language and having the languages we do possess recognized as valuable and acceptable. Staff can help children to feel good about themselves through valuing and extending their languages.

Staff/carers' checklist

The following checklist (Clarke 1991) could be used to determine whether your programme supports the development of language in all the children.

Indicator	Comment here
1 *Attitudes staff show towards children and families*	
Do we accept the use of the children's home languages in the programme?	☐
Do we expect too much of the children as they are learning English?	☐
Do we expect the parents to be able to speak English?	☐
Do we respect the individual child's needs and abilities?	☐
Is there evidence of languages other than English in the programme?	☐
2 *Interaction with EAL children*	
Do we respond to non-verbal as well as verbal language?	☐
Do we accept that some children may remain silent?	☐
Do we use a variety of question forms?	☐
Do we provide enough time for children to answer?	☐
Do we encourage other children to make time for EAL learners to respond?	☐
Do we use routine language?	☐
Are rich language experiences available outdoors as well as indoors?	☐
3 *Arrangements made for staff to work individually or in small groups with children*	
Are regular staff meetings held to discuss staff allocation?	☐
Is a mix of group times planned on a daily basis?	☐
Are groups scheduled every day in home languages for children?	☐
Are the rooms arranged to provide opportunities for children to have quiet times or work on an individual basis?	☐
4 *Efforts made to help children develop listening skills*	
Is music played constantly as a background so that children 'tune out' rather than 'tuning in'?	☐
Are listening games played?	☐
Do we demonstrate good models of listening?	☐

Do we encourage all children to demonstrate good models of
  listening? ☐
Do we sing songs in a range of languages? ☐

5 *Materials provided for children in both the home languages and
   English*
   Do children have regular opportunities to listen to stories and
     songs in their home languages? ☐
   Are bilingual staff employed? ☐
   Is there a multilingual lending library for parents and children? ☐
   Do we provide information for parents in their own languages? ☐
   Are we aware of assistance available from ethnic and community
     organizations? ☐

6 *Observing and assessing children's language development*
   Do we observe and record children's language development on
     a regular basis? ☐
   If assessments are needed to be made are these done in both
     languages? ☐
   Do we discuss our concerns with other staff, including bilingual
     staff? ☐
   Are parents regularly kept up to date with their children's
     progress? ☐
   Are assessments descriptive rather than prescriptive? ☐

Further reading

Ashworth, M. and Wakefield, H.P. (1994) *Teaching the World's Children: ESL for Ages Three to Seven*. Ontario: Pippin Publishing Ltd.

Clarke, P. (1992) *English as a Second Language in Early Childhood*. Melbourne, Victoria: Victoria Free Kindergarten Association.

Tabors, P.O. (1997) *One Child, Two Languages: A Guide for Preschool Educators of Children Learning English as a Second Language*. Baltimore, MD: Paul Brookes Publishing.

4

Diversity and the curriculum

Figure 4.1   Young children can gain first-hand experience of different cultures

Introduction

In this chapter we use the word programme to mean all the routines and procedures of an early childhood setting, including the curriculum. We refer to the curriculum as the planned areas of learning and all the staff and child initiated activities which contribute to learning and which are assessed, observed and recorded. Effective early childhood programmes provide children with a range of first-hand experiences that promote interactive learning, foster children's self-esteem and support individual children in their construction of knowledge. They also recognize the key role of play in young children's development and learning. Central to this is the role of the early childhood staff in establishing the learning environment, structuring interactions and supporting learners in their development.

Young, developing children do not compartmentalize their learning, so an integrated environment suitable for the development of cognitive, social, emotional, aesthetic, linguistic/communicative and physical dimensions needs to be created. All children have the right to an early childhood curriculum that supports and affirms their gender, cultural and linguistic identities and backgrounds. From an early age, young children are beginning to construct their identity and self-concept and this early development is influenced by the way that others view them and respond to them and their family. Within today's society, the prejudice and racist attitudes displayed towards children and families can influence their attitudes towards themselves and others (MacPherson 1999). Early childhood educators need to examine their own attitudes and prejudices and learn to deal with them in positive ways.

Our book does not refer to any particular guidelines for a set curriculum because across various countries guidelines differ. However, the content of this book would fit neatly into any of these guidelines. Similarly the UK *Desirable Outcomes* (SCAA 1996) guidance which has recently been developed into the *Early Learning Goals* does not specifically mention a curriculum for equity, but it assumes that cross-curricula themes will be pervasive. Neither are staff told 'how' to work with children. We see absolutely no reason why our aims and practical advice for strengthening the language and equity aspects of any early years curriculum would detract from any of the aims enshrined in any of these documents. All of that said, there is one set of curricula guidance worth mentioning briefly that has been developed by practitioners for practitioners.

A UK curriculum model: Quality in Diversity in Early Learning (QDEL)

The Quality in Diversity framework has recently been formulated by practitioners working in groups and a project team convened by the Early Childhood Education Forum (ECEF) in the UK. The curriculum guidelines, for those working with children from birth to 7 years, therefore represents a major collaboration between representatives of all of the major national organizations concerned with the care and education of young children. Grounded in principles drawn from Te Whariki, the New Zealand curriculum for the early years, the framework emphasizes the need to achieve quality provision for children of 'different abilities, dispositions, aptitudes and needs'. The context assumed is a diverse range of settings that cater for the diverse needs of a multicultural, multilingual and multifaith society. The greatest strength of the framework will undoubtably be in providing an auditing tool in the development of practice. One of the declared intentions has been to support practitioners in making comparisons between different curricular approaches, so that 'Selected observations could be made to enable practitioners to identify and justify the diversity in their practice of quality' (ECEF 1998: 8).

The framework provides guidance on three main elements: foundations, goals and entitlements. Whereas the foundations and goals relate most closely to policy and curriculum practice, it is the area of entitlement that relates most closely to pedagogy. The aim here has been to describe the conditions considered essential for early learning and to define a basic entitlement for learning support.

Parental partnership is emphasized and, as in all other programmes, play is considered crucial to early learning. There is a clear recognition of the need for adults to support and extend the children in their play. Children are also entitled to have their learning planned, resourced and organized as well as to have their progress understood and recorded. The importance of teachers observing children in their play and of evaluating and adapting what they do to maximize learning is emphasized.

The practitioners' wheel is provided to represent the favoured pedagogic practice. The concentric circles show the foundations of learning, and around these are the practitioners' daily tasks. The outer rim of the wheel shows the sources of information and evidence that the practitioners draw upon in their daily practice.

Much of the specific pedagogic guidance is embedded and little explicit reference is made to the quality of adult–child interactions. Some of the observations do, however, provide hints regarding the favoured specific adult roles. At times it seems to be one emphasizing a low profile and at

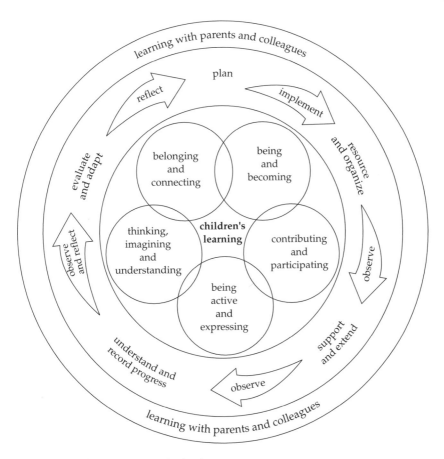

Figure 4.2 The practitioners' wheel
Source: Early Childhood Education Forum (1998)

others a high degree of direction. At one point we hear of two adults who 'took little part' in managing an activity as 'the children were very much in control' (ECEF 1998: 22). In another example the staff developed a whole series of supported investigations and other activities in response to questions that a group of children had asked about snails (1998: 56). This kind of flexibility seems entirely appropriate to us. We see the arguments that we make in this book for an inclusive curriculum entirely compatible with the aims of the QDEL guidelines. However, the knowledge and skills of many practitioners in playgroups, day nurseries, etc., are limited in the areas of equity and diversity, and we offer the rest of this chapter as a practical guide to developing this area of work. We are very much concerned with both valuing children and with making children feel secure enough to access areas of the curriculum, such as early literacy, numeracy and scientific concepts in a culturally appropriate and supportive environment.

All early childhood programmes should reflect multicultural and equity perspectives regardless of whether they are developed for exclusively English-speaking children or for children from a range of diverse backgrounds and languages. A culturally responsive curriculum and staff who understand and respect the cultural and linguistic backgrounds of the children in their care can make a difference. Children can grow up with the ability to retain their home language and culture and to have pride in their gender and class identity as well as adapting to the new cultures and languages of any early childhood setting they enter.

Curriculum for children in the early years should:

- foster children's self-esteem;
- acknowledge the cultural and linguistic backgrounds of all children;
- actively maintain and develop the children's first or home languages;
- promote the learning of English as an additional language;
- value bilingualism as an asset;
- value what boys and girls can do equally;
- support families in their efforts to maintain their languages and culture;
- foster an awareness of diversity in class, gender, ability and culture;
- promote respect for similarity and difference;
- challenge bias and prejudice;
- promote a sense of fairness;
- promote principles of inclusion and equity;
- support the participation of the parents in the children's learning.

Curriculum for children under 3 years

The first year of life is crucial for young children to acquire 'basic trust' (Erikson 1950). This is a feeling of safety and security in the world around them. Basic trust comes from the provision of responsive care in a supportive, predictable environment that enables children to develop positive relationships with others (see Hurst and Joseph 1998).

In planning a curriculum for babies and toddlers from diverse backgrounds, Milne (1993: 13) highlights essential criteria that need to be taken into consideration. Children need:

- responsive and responsible caregivers that they can trust;
- a physically safe, warm, consistent, predictable environment with stable routines, equipment, faces and places;

- freedom to explore challenges and freedom to ignore them;
- verbal and non-verbal communication.

Cook and Porter (1996: 29) suggest the following strategies for staff in designing spaces for babies and toddlers:

- offer a variety of materials and freedom for children to reject materials which are not culturally acceptable or familiar;
- arrange play spaces to give clear non-verbal communication about the expectations adults have for children;
- provide spaces for close interactions between staff and children;
- provide quiet spaces for individuals and small groups;
- arrange sleeping places so as to provide babies and toddlers with some familiar objects and practices.

Staff working with babies and toddlers need to be particularly sensitive to issues of diversity. Consideration needs to be given to the particular child-rearing practices practised at home, and the beliefs, goals and values that lie behind them. These cross-cultural issues will affect the way young children settle into care, and we refer to this in greater depth in the chapter dealing with parent partnerships. For the time being, issues to consider include:

Attachment and separation

For young children, one of the most important needs is to attach to at least one person. Obviously the most important attachment is at home and most children already have an attachment to an adult when they begin child care or nursery. For babies and toddlers from diverse backgrounds, forming a new attachment is more difficult in a new environment where staff look and speak differently and where the routines and play situations are completely foreign (Gonzales-Mena 1998).

The settling in period for children new to childcare and education settings is vital. The following strategies (adapted from Cockram and Cook 1994) can be used to facilitate this process for children from diverse backgrounds:

- encourage parents to visit with their children on several occasions before leaving them for the first time;
- encourage parents to explain the events of the day to their child in their own language;
- try to understand the parents' perspective and concerns for leaving their children for the first time;
- suggest to parents that they make the first few occasions when children are left short;

- suggest that parents say goodbye, tell the child where they are going and when they will return, for example, after sleep;
- encourage the parents to leave something of their own for the child to care for in their absence;
- provide bilingual support for the child;
- allocate a particular staff member to remain with the child;
- make sure parents leave a phone number where they can be contacted during the day;
- provide play materials which are familiar;
- find out the routines of the child.

Sleeping patterns

Adults, even from the same culture, do not always agree with the way children are put to sleep in childcare settings, and families from different cultural backgrounds may also have different patterns for sleeping (Gonzales-Mena 1993). In some cultures, sleeping is an intimate time when children sleep with parents and siblings; the child may be breast-fed prior to sleep, or cuddled and sung to (Cook and Porter 1996). Some families may be used to a routine time for sleeping, whereas others may encourage their children to sleep when they are tired. Discussion with parents will provide information about sleeping preferences of the children and the wishes of the parents. In the initial days it may be possible to provide sleeping arrangements that are more like those the child is used to.

Meals and snacktime

Food and meal times are a central part of all cultures. Cook and Porter (1996: 3–4) suggest that staff in early childhood settings need to consider the home experiences of children and the level of match or discrepancy in children starting in childcare. The following are worth considering:

- the routine of breastfeeding and introduction of solids;
- the choice of staple foods that children are used to;
- the value placed on independence versus dependence;
- the creative and spiritual aspects of food – including wasting food, play with food and food taboos;
- the eating styles and preferences.

Toileting

The toilet training of toddlers varies across different cultures and the times considered appropriate for starting this may also vary. Be aware of the way young children have been trained by parents to use toilet facilities. For example, some children may be taught to stand or squat on the seat. Some parents may not like communal toilets for girls and boys together.

Dressing

There are many different styles of dressing and some children may be dressed more formally for childcare than other families. For some cultures, clothes are very important and religions may require the wearing of long pants, scarves and head-dresses. Parents' wishes for their children must be respected and all staff and children encouraged to understand the diversity in the community. Sometimes other children in the group may be curious about differences in dress and make remarks. It is important to talk with children about the differences in the way some people dress.

At a pre-school in Melbourne several children drew attention to the head scarf worn by a mother and child, originally from Malaysia. The mother was happy to come and explain to the children why she covered her head, she showed how the scarf was folded and provided one for the children to have in the home corner. For several days, the children dressed up in it during their play. However, one must not assume that every parent will want to do this.

Touch and contact

The use of gestures, touch and contact are ways of communicating that may vary according to different cultures. It is important that staff find out and respect the different styles, as parents can be offended by certain actions of staff, such as making direct eye contact or touching the heads of children. The best thing to do is to engage parents in friendly conversations and when trust has been established to ask direct questions about any differences which staff do not fully understand.

Some parents also are uncomfortable when they see their babies and toddlers being undressed in front of strangers or in a public place. It is important to discuss these issues with the families and find out what they are used to. It may be necessary to use an interpreter to explain, and to accommodate a parent's needs within, the routine procedures of the centre.

Curriculum for children from 3 to 6 years

As with the younger children, pre-school children in the early years need access to a good quality programme that supports their cultural and linguistic development. As has been discussed in previous chapters, the home language and culture play a critical role in children's overall development, and children from varying cultural backgrounds have access to different language and socialization experiences of gender and class. As the nursery or reception class is often the first institutional setting for the children, it is essential that a bridge is formed between the language and cultural practices of the home and community and the new environment of the school.

In the early years setting the daily curriculum provides a balance between regular routines, activities and spontaneous child–adult and child–child interactions. In certain regular situations (for example, storytime, small group games) the teacher's behaviour and language provides clues for children learning English. The children can associate what they hear with visual images. Both the children and the adults in the nursery tend to support their talk with concrete objects, actions and social events that are present in the immediate context.

It cannot be assumed that all children will learn at the same pace within the early childhood setting. The contexts of each early childhood setting will vary and different influences will be present at different times, which will in turn provide different opportunities for children to interact. In any situation there are individual differences that affect the way young children learn. Staff have an important role in encouraging children's development and in maximizing the learning environment. They need to be able to respond to the individual needs of the learners as some learners may find it harder to understand what is going on and may have difficulty settling into an environment very different from the home.

In setting up the nursery or pre-school environment to support children's development, children need opportunities:

- to observe and listen to others;
- to try to make sense of what they see and hear;
- to practise what they know and can do;
- to experiment with language – both the first language and English;
- to interact with others and share experiences.

In the next part of this chapter, the key elements of the early years programme that support interaction are discussed.

Encouraging interaction and involvement

The environment should be prepared in such a way that it encourages children to be actively involved with it. The key elements of planning should include:

Time

Early childhood staff need to consider the time that is allowed for aspects of the day and to plan for arrivals and departures, routine and transition times, resting, playing, group times and pack away times. Children's ability to adjust to the different aspects of the day may be influenced by their class and cultural background and by previous experiences. It is essential to discuss these issues with parents in order to establish what the young child is familiar with. Older children need long stretches of uninterrupted time to sustain constructive play, and to have time to become engrossed in the activities and concentrate on complete tasks.

Children with English as an additional language need to be encouraged to use their home languages at this time. They may need to be supported by bilingual, bicultural staff so that they get the opportunity to communicate what they know and what they want. For these children, not only is the language used in the environment unfamiliar, but the experiences, materials and routines are unfamiliar. They need support to adjust to this. Staff need to be sensitive to the individual needs of the children and adapt periods of time to suit the play that is developing. Although routine times are also important, particularly for children from different cultural backgrounds entering a new language environment, time allowed for children's play can be flexible.

Space

The arrangement of the space in the early childhood setting should be based on what staff know about the way children develop and their interactional needs. The space should allow for young children to learn through active involvement in their environment; they should also have opportunities to be alone. The provision of a stimulating and challenging environment should provide opportunities for children to make choices and decisions.

In planning the environment, staff need to consider the safety and supervision of the children when considering how they will place equipment and materials to support children's interaction. In particular they need to decide:

- the arrangement of equipment, materials and spaces both inside and outside;
- the balance between enclosed spaces and open spaces;
- the type of boundaries between different areas;
- the way materials will be grouped;
- the provision of free movement in the playroom;

- the opportunity for quiet reflective times;
- the opportunity for physical play;
- the safety and supervision of the children.

The way the indoor and outdoor space is arranged will convey messages about the value placed on the culture and language backgrounds of the families. The layout of the playroom or classroom affects children's emotional security and ability to choose free play. Children need sufficient space to play effectively. Too many early years settings are cramped with tables and chairs and furniture, or with activities that are too closely predetermined, such as work sheets. Research shows that when the amount of space is decreased, children exhibit more aggressive and less social play behaviour (Rogers and Sawyers 1988). In addition, the way the space is set up impacts on the type and nature of children's interactions. In planning spaces for children, staff need to think clearly about the placement of well defined and well resourced interest centres; unobstructed access to materials should be provided and attention should be given to the display of pictures, posters and other wall decorations that reflect diversity.

Consider both the indoor and outdoor environments. The outdoor environment is often neglected. Both areas should be planned to maximize interactions and provide for play. The way the playroom is organized should provide many opportunities for young learners to interact in small groups, on a one-to-one basis with another child or an adult, or in small groups. The setting should allow children to experience quiet times as well as activities that encourage talk. An effective programme requires the provision of a supportive environment with well defined play areas, materials and equipment.

Learning through play

Play is highly valued in the early years for its ability to stimulate and integrate a wide range of children's intellectual, physical, cultural, social and creative abilities. As Milne (1997: 7) states 'a lot of what is called educational play in early childhood is neither play nor education. It is not play in a rich sense if it is dominated by an adult; neither is it education in a rich sense if it lacks any adult guidance.' Play has a high degree of self-motivation, free choice and spontaneity. The type of play most valued in the early years is imaginative or 'symbolic' play. Symbolic play is play in which one thing is used to stand for or represent another. The following examples demonstrate this:

Anna (3 years 6 months) and Vicki (3 years 6 months) are playi
home corner at a nursery. They have two large cartons:

> *Anna:* Say this is your bed, mum, and this one is mine.
> *Vicki:* No. Mine's the TV. Here's the new TV Dad.
> *Anna:* OK. Where does the TV go Mum?

The gender role-playing that is going on here is also using a form of symbolism – Vicki represents a 'mum' and Anna a 'dad' (Milne 1990). In separating what it is that Mums and Dads signify and 'do' from their concrete experience of them in the real world, the children are able to explore and experiment with the roles in a more abstract and intellectual way. Even younger children, without verbal language also display the capacity for symbolic functioning.

Children from language backgrounds other than English symbolize a varity of experiences from their own cultural backgrounds. Con (17 months) walks up to a piece of crumpled white paper on the floor. He spreads it out, then lies down, positioning the paper as if it were a pillow. Con screws his eyes up. He opens them and looks up at the caregiver, then closes them again. After this he gets up and wanders off. Here Con is not only using the paper to symbolize an object – a pillow, he is also using his own body to symbolize the action of going to sleep (Milne 1990).

Nasra, a young Panjabi-speaking 3-year-old was walking around the nursery. She had a block to her ear and was talking loudly in Urdu as she walked up and down the room. Later the Urdu-speaking bilingual teacher was asking her about the conversation:

> *Member of staff:* (*in Urdu*) I saw you having a long conversation on the phone today, who were you talking to?
> *Nasra:* (*in Urdu*) I had to ring dad. He'd gone to the market and we needed more rice for the pilaf. He said he'd be late.
> *Member of staff:* Were you cooking the pilaf?
> *Nasra:* I'm the mum, Sharif's the dad and he's gone to the market.

Even though Nasra had limited English, her ability to use her home experiences and language was supported by the bilingual staff member. This type of play is instrumental in the development of internal systems of representation and abstract thought. The representations gradually free children from their early reliance on shared experiences and allow them to think about objects and events that are not immediately present and to think about the past and plan ahead for the future (Clarke 1996).

's the young child's development of symbolic rep-
rly use of objects in play to stand for or represent
ansion of oral language as a form of symbolic rep-
he gradual understanding by the child of the sym-
?. According to Vygotsky (1978), imaginative play
rm at a higher level because the context of imag-
ched to the forms of knowing of young children.
children, in the imaginative play context, to reach
their immediate knowledge of the 'here and now' and the expres-
sion of meanings through symbols. Within the early years context, such
play is traditionally encouraged by the provision of space, time, properties
and adult support.

In a major review of research on the relationship between symbolic play
and early literacy Schrader (1990) supports Vygotsky's earlier claim that
symbolic play is the perfect tool for literacy development. She suggests that
the most useful interventions are those where the adult participates in play
within the framework of the child players, then extends it sensitively from
within rather than planning or directing it externally. The adult has an
important role as a participant in play rather than directing it. Rather than
taking over the play, the adult becomes just one of the players, encouraging
children to contribute their ideas and directions to the play (Am 1986).

The current emphasis on the importance of early literacy has seen a
growing movement away from play-based programmes in the early years
to more structured programmes that rely heavily on instruction and see
children as passive recipients waiting to be filled up with knowledge. This
is especially so for children in the 4–6 age group. Gardner (1991) argues
that play is the creative process that gives birth to literacy. Literacy is about
the understanding of symbols. Symbols are things that can represent
something else – an object, event or idea. Words are symbols. Thinking
skills involve the manipulation of symbols of many different kinds: words,
numbers, images, notations. Therefore, early literacy foundations are not
necessarily primarily about books and stories.

Early literacy foundations are primarily about talking and playing.
Exposure to print and reading and writing come later. In the early years,
play is the first medium for practice in creating and manipulating symbols
and representations of many different kinds. Children create or use symbols in their drawing, painting, block constructions, make-believe play,
clay modelling, finger plays, 'cubby' house buildings, carpentry, storytime, sand, water and dress-ups and many other activities.

During play, children's use of language is more complex than in most
other activities. They use greater vocabulary and they use longer utterances than they do in most other situations. Later literacy is built on the

foundation of solid language development in the early years (Almy 1988). Interactive and collaborative play provides rich opportunities for young children learning English as an additional language to learn and practise language. Children learn to use English in communication with others because they want to develop relationships with others, and play situations provide real motivation for working at extending their tools of communication.

The role of play in an early childhood curriculum may be a concept that some minority ethnic families and those from different class backgrounds find hard to understand. Fleer (1999: 73) reminds us that in multicultural communities it cannot be assumed that western theories of play are relevant for all children. Much of the literature on play is derived from research conducted from a western perspective and collected in western contexts. In some cultures, play is valued highly. In other cultures, play is not regarded seriously. Culture helps to determine whether play is something children do on their own or whether adult participation is valued. As Milne (1997: 35) states, 'we need to recognize the strong cultural influences of values. Different cultural attitudes towards play in early education may have justifications that are not always apparent to those who don't fully understand their roots.'

The challenge for early childhood educators is to be aware of the different cultural values and expectations held by parents, of how these beliefs affect their children and affect their attitude to the child care. It is important to understand that some families will be settling into a new country, other families who are second or third generation may also retain some of their old values and customs but others will be modified and some will disappear altogether. Early childhood staff need to be respectful of other childrearing practices yet still be professional and share their knowledge and expertise. The process is a two-way one, which needs staff and families to work together to decide what can be accommodated and what is best for the children (Siraj-Blatchford 1994a,b).

A number of researchers have affirmed the importance of play in the acquisition of the second language in young children. In her study of 3-year-olds, Nemoianu (1980: 15) claimed that children learn a second language faster and with less effort during play if they are motivated to establish friendships with peers. Play provides the focus for interaction, and because young children want to interact with others, they need to use language. Like Nemoianu, Wong-Fillmore (1976) also recognized the importance of children's desires to establish social relationships through play. She argued that children hear many well-contextualized phrases that are repetitious in nature and therefore easy to learn. Using these phrases, learners can quickly become part of the social group.

Children's play is enhanced by the richness of their life experiences and their ability to communicate their own ideas and listen to the ideas of others. Children may or may not need an adult to facilitate this play depending on how good their communication and social skills are (Creaser 1989: 59). Some children in the nursery or early years settings, find it hard to make friends with others and join in play because they do not share a common language or because they find it difficult to communicate their own ideas. Research has indicated that children who are rejected by their peers tend to feel lonely and isolated. These children may miss out on opportunities to develop social skills that are essential for later learning.

Research in some English-speaking countries with diverse populations has shown that children from different cultural and linguistic backgrounds who had limited English found it difficult to take part in sociodramatic play with English-speaking children without the support of staff. Sometimes other English-speaking children tried to assist but they were unable to sustain the interactions for long. Results showed that for children with limited English, the teacher was needed to intervene in their play and encourage the learners in their use of English (Fraser and Wakefield 1986; Clarke 1996). However, children also need the opportunity to use their first language to take part in free play. Research (Clarke 1996) shows that when bilingual children use their home language in sociodramatic play, the language used in these play situations is much more complex than the situations in which the children use English, even when the teacher tries to scaffold the play. Children who have the opportunity to use their home language in play situations have greater cognitive flexibility and can build on knowledge gained through the first language. This has interesting implications for the rest of the curriculum when bilingual children may be engaged in art, science or construction activities. Staff have to plan carefully for supporting children's learning in a range of groupings and with a range of support in both the home language and English.

Early childhood staff have a critical role in planning an environment which encourages children's learning through play. Staff need to be aware of providing a wide variety of opportunities for all children, regardless of social class, ability, gender, language and culture, and even challenging children to cross gender or cultural boundaries through play (MacNaughton 1999). Staff need to facilitate this play by encouraging children to join in with their peers and supporting the interactions without controlling them. In other types of play such as formal rule games, the staff role may include much more direction, modelling both the structure of the play and the language of the game.

A teacher is playing a card game with two children:

> *Teacher:* Where's a card with four on? I can see one.
> (*Abdul points to one in front of him*)
> *Abdul (4 years):* Here one.
> *Teacher:* Good shot. How many ladybirds did you find?
> *William (4 years):* There's three on my card. I can count them, one, two, three.
> *Abdul:* Me too.
> *Teacher:* That's right. Can you find a card that's got three. Look over there in that pile. Good, that's right. We can match them up now.
> (*The children reach and match the cards to the boards they have*)

During play, children need opportunities for interaction with both children and adults. Adult–child interactions may be more free-flowing than child–child interactions. However, as they take place between more or less equal partners who have an investment in the ongoing conversation, peer conversations have the potential to support language development. As children take part in conversations they learn and practise the rules of talk: listening, turn-taking and keeping to the topic. Through interaction with others they pick up cues to conversation, recognize breaks in conversation, know how to add information, and how to make themselves heard. For children with English as an additional language these skills have been learned in their first language. They bring this knowledge about language to the new language environment.

Research has shown that peers can assist learners to maintain conversations by using non-verbal cues and routines, by repeating previous utterances and by extending the functions of their English vocabulary and grammar.

When Joshua (3 years 6 months) started in the nursery he was very anxious to play with the other children. However, he had very little English and there were no other Somali-speakers in the group. Initially he hung back, but when the teacher saw him watching she suggested to Ali (4 years) and Mahmoud (3 years 6 months) that they might like Joshua to join in their play. The teacher selected a new picture lotto game from her store cupboard and invited the children to join her. This game provided opportunities for Joshua to imitate the words and actions of Ali and Mahmoud as they all matched the pictures held up by the teacher. Joshua was able to work out the meanings from the context.

The next day, the teacher encouraged Ali and Mahmoud to invite Joshua to join their play in the sand pit. She helped them talk through ideas about what they were proposing and encouraged Ali and Mahmoud to take

m to the shed to choose props for their play. This peer play
it encourages the development of social skills while pro-
nities to learn language and practise new forms in ways
negotiation and turn-taking.

the importance of social interaction has been highlighted.

has emphasized the need for encouraging the develop-
ment of social skills and of supporting young children in their attempts at
interacting with others.

Adult-directed, structured or scaffolded play

Many opportunities exist in the early childhood setting for structured
adult-directed play. These include the provision of activities in which the
adult plays a major role in the interactions. Other adult-directed play can
occur in group times which include the provision of games with rules,
card games, matching games and outdoor games with balls. Since many of
these activities require adult direction, the children hear a great deal of
natural language directed to the 'here and now', such as instructions for
playing the game, rules of turn-taking and new information. In these
activities the materials to be used make the behavioural and language
expectations clear and simple for the children. The way the games are
organized and the support provided by staff assist the learners to take part
using the comprehension and level of English they know at that time. For
example, in matching games such as picture lotto, children can join in
using non-verbal actions only.

A mix of group times should be planned for inclusion in the daily programme. These should include opportunities for the whole group of children to meet for singing, games and music; small groups of three or four
children to take part in card games, matching or stories; groups with eight
or ten children for cooking, stories or discussions. The way groups are
structured is important for children learning English as a second language, and for social class and gender mixing. Wherever possible children
who can already speak English should be included, not only to provide
other English language models but also to encourage more English use
between the learners and their friends.

Small group activities (Clarke 1999) are valuable for all children
because:

- they have more opportunities to participate when there are fewer of
  them to compete for staff attention;
- the smaller number of children in the group make it easier for staff
  to provide information that is easily understood;
- the smaller number of children makes it easier for staff to respond to

individual requests and not provide more or less attention to boys or girls;

- the staff can pause and wait longer for children to respond;
- the staff can model and expand the limited English or single words used by the learners;
- the children can understand more easily and there are less distractions;
- the children have more chance to get to know others;
- the groups provide opportunities for staff to assess children's individual needs.

Many of the games that encourage communication can be played bilingually, in the home language or in English. Children's language development can be facilitated at these group times by an adult, for example involving a bilingual staff member, parent or a child with more English proficiency. Children can be paired together for games. Staff can use the children's interaction in these games to observe the children's language and assess their level of comprehension and skill with English. These activities provided scope for learners to respond in their own way and at their own pace without making rigid demands on them. Even if children respond only with non-verbal gestures, their limited responses can still be viewed as them taking some part as the following example shows:

A staff member is playing 'Kim's game' with two children. She has some objects on a tray and she covers them with a cloth. Each time before she takes the cloth off she removes an item. The children name the item. However, Fatima does not say anything.

Adult: What did I take away?
Mahmoud (3 years 6 months): The key.
Adult: Well done, I can't trick you.
Adult: Now it's Fatima's turn. Fatima?
    (*Fatima doesn't answer*)
Adult: Was it the book?
    (*Fatima shakes her head*)
Adult: No, that's right. Was it the block?
    (*Fatima shakes her head*)
Mahmoud: It's a orange
Adult: That's right. Well done. It's an orange.

The scaffolding routines used by staff to assist children to participate in games and activities are much more predominant in adult-directed activities than in child-centred activities. The following activities and games are beneficial for all young learners:

- picture lotto;
- snap and other card games;
- sequential cards;
- children's board games like snakes and ladders;
- counting games;
- activities such as cutting and pasting in which the staff work on a one-to-one basis with children;
- puzzles and jigsaws.

Games such as these provide opportunities for children to put things into sequence, to sort and classify, to label, describe and match objects, to ask and answer questions and to take turns. They can be played in English, in languages other than English or bilingually. They provide all children with opportunities to learn something of another language.

When selecting games for children it is very important to choose games with pictures reflecting the diversity in the community. At the same time stereotypes should be avoided. Illustrations can provide a means of introducing children to possibilities that may be under-realized in their local environment. For example, illustrations may be selected that depict women and men, girls and boys in a variety of roles. For example, girls fixing a bicycle, women as engineers, men working with young children. Illustrations should also reflect ability and disability, ethnicity and religious differences. But, as always, it is very important that these images do not further add to stereotypes.

Materials

Children need to have access to a wide range of materials to stimulate and support their play. These materials should be well organized and readily accessible. Materials for sociodramatic play should reflect mixed gender roles, cultural diversity and encourage all children to interact with others. The range of materials should include recycled material as well as commercial toys and games. Some children may need to be assisted to use materials.

The outdoors can provide stimuli for dramatic play such as low tables, cushions, outdoor markets with baskets and mats, a place for preparing, cooking and eating food outdoors. Make signs 'girls at work', signs for road construction, etc. Provide implements and containers for sand play outdoors – sieves, strainers, wok, pans, cooking trays, muffin tins and piping. Make sure your sandpit is accessible for children with a disability. Provide a piece of mat or a box for children to sit on if they do not like to sit on the sand.

These are just a few suggestions, discuss them with staff in your nursery, share ideas with colleagues in other areas. Visit local markets and shops to get ideas of what you might include in your environment. See Chapter 7 on resources to help practitioners plan the curriculum.

Ensuring the curriculum supports diversity

In the early years, the children's learning is facilitated by a range of play materials that support their individual needs including culture, language, gender and ability. In considering the resources needed, the activities initiated in the centre provide a starting point for deciding what can be achieved. This includes the environment indoors and the variety of experiences outdoors.

Staff in the early years need to ask themselves how their service is perceived by people from diverse backgrounds. Does the curriculum reflect the social class, education, gender, culture and language of the community it serves? All areas of the nursery and school should support the diversity of the children and families who attend and should encourage all children to develop positive feelings towards others. The following list provides some ideas for resources that can be provided in all areas of the indoor and outdoor environment.

Home corner

Provide a range of dolls reflecting diversity; include food packages, tins, boxes and packets that have labels in other languages; wall hangings, rugs, lengths of material for dressing up, trousers, caps, bag, baby slings and carriers, chopsticks, bowls, etc. Change this area frequently to raise the children's curiosity and level of play. Home corners can become Indian restaurants, cafes, dental surgery, travel agency, newsagents or a hospital.

Consider encouraging children to set up their own houses (cubbies) outdoors. Provide a cloth, outdoor blocks, pieces of matting, lengths of wood. Encourage children to construct a shelter themselves.

Puzzles and manipulative equipment

Ensure that this equipment reflects realistic images of diversity – able/disabled, religious, cultural, gay and lesbian couples, markets, shopping centres, occupations, activities, hobbies and leisure time. Remember to avoid foreign or exotic images, these can only encourage stereotypes. Staff should use these resources themselves before the children use them to anticipate and reflect on the types of questions children might raise. These questions can then be discussed amongst staff to ensure a consistent response to children.

Music and singing

Staff should provide a variety of music activities that provide opportunities for children to listen to music and to join in. These should include:

- a listening post (tape recorder and headphones) with a selection of tapes – stories in languages other than English and in English, rhymes and poems, classical music, nursery songs, dance music, music from different cultures, percussion;
- use of singing to accompany activities;
- regular group times – sometimes with all the children to provide security for some children, plan smaller groups to encourage children to talk, plan group times for percussion, dancing and movement to music.

Encourage bilingual staff and parents to share songs and rhymes from their cultures. Put them together into your own nursery songbook. Add favourite songs and rhymes in English and give a copy of the book to each family to enjoy at home.

Books, book corner, children's and parents' library

Books are an important part of the nursery and school and can be crucial in reinforcing both negative and positive feelings and attitudes. In selecting books for children it is important to consider the illustrations, story line, language, cultural issues, gender, class and ability stereotypes. The following publications are helpful in developing criteria for the selection of books:

Celestin, N. (1986) *A Guide to Anti-Racist Child Care Practice.* London: Voluntary Organizations Liaison Council for Under-fives.
Neugebauer, B. (1992) *Alike and Different: Exploring our Humanity with Young Children.* Washington DC: NAEYC.
Siraj-Blatchford, I. (1994a) *The Early Years: Laying the Foundations for Racial Equality.* Stoke-on-Trent: Trentham Books.

See also Chapter 7.

Have books on display all the time

A book corner is essential for providing opportunities for children to read for themselves or read to others. If staff find time to sit in this corner and share books on a one-to-one or small group basis this provides wonderful exposure to a range of books. The book corner or shelf should include a range of books.

Set up a bilingual library for children and parents

A bilingual library offers children and parents the opportunity to share the same books, audio tapes and compact discs that children have used at nursery or school. Parents are often willing to assist in distributing the books and keeping the loan system up to date. If your nursery or school does not have much money to purchase books for this library, think of making simple books which children can illustrate, make collections of favourite songs, ask parents to write out the words of songs in languages other than English.

Other everyday areas like the block area, can provide space for the display of posters, illustrations, photographs of people, buildings, transport.

Storytime

In listening to a story, children need to have the opportunity to hear a range of stories in their first or home languages. The stories provided should be supported by clear illustrations and the text should be simple and unambiguous. If possible, children should have the opportunity to have had prior exposure to the vocabulary and some of the structures used in the story.

Selecting books and other reading materials

Provide a range of different types of books and other reading materials from which children may choose: factual, picture storybooks, bilingual books, books about families from different cultures, fantasy, poetry, rhymes and nonsense, books with audio tapes, big books, homemade books. Ensure that the storybooks chosen have clear illustrations which provide the children with very good cues to the story line and the sequence of events (see also the Resources section at the end of the book).

Keep the session short

Some children new to English may find it difficult to sit for long periods of time listening to stories in English. Choose books that can be told or read in a short space of time. If the book is long, consider telling it and shortening it at appropriate places, or consider reading it in two parts, recapping the first part when reading the second part.

Consider the size of the group

The best storytime is a shared time when children have the opportunity to take part and join in the discussion. If possible try to include children who already speak some English. Use parents and bilingual staff to read stories to children in their own language. This may be the same stories used in English or other stories.

Staff checklist

The following checklist may assist you to develop a supportive and interactive play environment.

Indicator	Yes	No	In the future
Is there a comfortable and stress free environment?			
Does the arrangement of the room encourage interaction?			
Are there opportunities for children to participate in a range of activities?			
Does the structure of the day provide opportunities for routine times and times for free play?			
Is enough time given for children to complete tasks?			
Are there opportunities for children to enjoy quiet times?			
Are staff familiar with the children's cultural and linguistic backgrounds?			
Does the environment reflect the cultural/language backgrounds of all the children?			
Are children encouraged to use their first or home languages?			
Are bilingual staff employed to support the children's use of their first languages?			
Are bilingual staff encouraged to develop resources in the first language (books, board games, song cards)?			
Are there regular group times in languages other than English?			

Are parents of children encouraged to
participate in the programme?
Are children given opportunities to
participate in interactions with their peers
and/or staff?
Do children participate in a range of groups
each day?
Does the equipment provided reflect
diversity?
Are there positive images of identity, gender,
ability, ethnicity, language and religion?
Do the books and posters portray girls and
boys in non-stereotypical roles?

Further reading

Duffy, B. (1998) *Supporting Creativity and Imagination in the Early Years*. Bucking-
ham: Open University Press.
Greenman, J. and Stonehouse, A. (1997) *Prime Times*. Melbourne, Victoria: Addison
Wesley Longman.
Lunt, C. and Williamson, D. (1999) *Children's Experiences Folio: Developmentally
Appropriate Experiences for 0-6 Years*. Melbourne, Victoria: RMIT Publishing.
Moyles, J. (ed.) (1994) *The Excellence of Play*. Buckingham: Open University Press.

5

Parents as partners

Figure 5.1 Finding out about a child's home background aids
continuity into the early years setting
Photograph: Sally Abbott Smith

Cross-cultural childrearing

Individual children bring their own unique characteristics to the early childhood environment. These characteristics have been influenced by their home environment, the wider community in which their families operate and the cultural and linguistic values held by their families. All families have very different expectations about the child's position in the family, the way the child speaks to other members of the family, and about the child as a member of the family setting. These differences may become more marked on entering an unfamiliar environment such as a nursery or childcare centre.

A number of researchers (Derman-Sparks 1992; Lubeck 1996) argue that the dominant culture of the European-American-centred classroom may be at odds with the learning styles and practices of minority ethnic children. Lubeck (1996: 20) urges educators to understand how early childhood practices help to maintain social inequality by creating status differentials between and among people and by reinforcing ideologies most likely to have been acquired by the dominant classes. Many studies have examined the discontinuities and continuities between the home and school experiences of children from diverse ethnic, racial, gender and social class groups (see Philips 1972, 1983), as well as between the difference of cultures children can experience in pre-school and schools (Heath 1982; Schofield 1982; Willett 1987). Observed cultural and gendered differences include: differences in non-verbal behaviours, dialect features of speech, accepted turn-taking practices and definitions of leading and following, adult and adult roles and adult and child roles, cooperation and competition.

In studies conducted by Heath (1982), she observed the way teachers built bridges so that the children could 'learn school'. For example, teachers upset with children who did not behave as they expected, learned to revise and clarify implicit definitions of how time and space were to be used in their classrooms. They also learned to express requests directly, while providing opportunities for children to learn mainstream forms through stories, puppets and other means.

Although early childhood educators play an important role in the care and education of children, they need to take account of what parents want for their own children. They should consider the diverse backgrounds of the families who are part of their programmes and they should work with parents to understand the cultural and linguistic values and goals parents have for their children. These are crucial to the identities of children, families and communities.

Children begin learning to be members of their own culture from birth.

They are exposed to culturally appropriate ways of behaving from an early age. This includes personal behaviour (the way we sit, stand, walk or gesture), interactional behaviour (personal space, eye contact, use of gestures, the rules followed, for example, good table and non-acceptable behaviour). Some aspects of the culture are more visible, including food, art, music, literature, festivals and important celebrations. Childrearing practices also differ and are often based on beliefs held by families over generations about what children need, how they should be handled, what girls and boys should or should not be able to do, how they learn and develop, and what personal characteristics should be learned.

In any early childhood programme, different cultures operate, and these include the different cultures of the children from diverse ethnic and cultural backgrounds as well as the home cultures of the staff. These all interplay with the culture of early childhood professional practice which is predominantly Anglo-European. But in recent years, this early childhood culture has begun to reflect other influences. The traditional 'developmentally appropriate curriculum' (Bredekamp 1987) has been revised to include three new areas of knowledge and practice. These consider what is developmentally appropriate, what is individually appropriate, and what is culturally appropriate. Gonzales-Mena (1998: 226) suggests that the early childhood culture is expanding beyond its European roots to increasingly reflect the diverse cultures of the many professional educators and the families they serve.

It is essential that those working with young children understand the conflict that is sometimes faced by very young children coming from diverse cultural backgrounds. One example of this is the different priorities families have in relation to independence or interdependence. Gonzales-Mena (1998) highlights the two major tasks newborn babies are faced with: 1) to become independent individuals and 2) to establish connections with others. The task of the parent is to help them with both. Their culture affects the way they address these tasks and determines the goals they have for their children. Gonzales-Mena (1998: 227) provides two approaches:

- the self is a separate, autonomous individual whose job it is to grow and develop into the best he or she can be in order to become part of a larger group. Personal fulfilment and/or achievement are all important.
- the self is inherently connected, not separate, and is defined in terms of relationships. Obligations to others is more important than personal fulfilment or achievement.

Difficulties may arise when young children are faced with conflicting expectations. The family may value interdependence, their major concern being to assist their children to maintain connections. They may worry about their children becoming too independent. On the other hand, the culture of the early childhood setting may value independence and encourage self-help skills. Problems may arise when parents expect their child to be fed at the childcare setting, as these meal times are seen as providing important opportunities for interaction between child and parent. Parents may be upset at the centre's policy to encourage children to become more independent.

Gonzales-Mena (1998: 229) argues that 'the independence and interdependence approaches represent two different ways of looking at getting needs met'. In different cultures, some children will grow up with a strong positive feeling of community that can provide support when they receive negative messages about themselves or about their communities.

What is important for early childhood educators is to recognize the different cultural influences that are present, to be accepting of other ways of viewing childrearing, to respect the ability of parents to raise their own children and to be aware of negative influences which can oppress people. This is important because self-esteem and identity depend on whether these factors are recognized and treated with respect. As children enter new environments, cultures change as do individuals. Children start from different cultural backgrounds, and whether they keep their cultural values or whether they are changed or lost altogether will depend partly on the ability of the early childhood staff to support the child's development. Ultimately it should be the children's decision as they grow older to decide what is of importance. However expert in terms of child development we may be, we should not presume to make decisions for them. In earlier chapters, positive ways of supporting children in early childhood programmes have been discussed.

Home culture and language

Even though families might have emigrated to a new country they bring with them the parenting and cultural roles that they have experienced themselves. These beliefs and values are reinforced, or depending on the experiences they have in the new country, may be changed or rejected as new generations are born. Although there may be similarities as well as differences across cultures, there will be differences in the way children have been exposed to ways of talking and listening, and parents may have clear expectations of the way children will use language, including who talks to whom, about what topics, and who responds.

Over the past 20 years, research in a variety of social and cultural communities has broadened our knowledge and understanding of specific cultural and linguistic patterns used by families and communities with varied sociocultural characteristics. Findings from research have shown complex patterns of language use, socialization patterns and learning. Pease-Alvarez and Vasquez (1994) and Clarke (1996) argue that the home language and culture plays a critical role in children's overall development and that people from different cultures have access to very different language socialization experiences. These experiences can result in different paths to second language learning.

Pease-Alvarez and Vasquez (1994) draw attention to the work of Heath (1983) and Schieffelin and Ochs (1986) who show that the way parents and other adults interact with children is influenced by the culturally-specific views about childrearing and language learning they hold. Middle-class white Anglo-European parents who believe that language learning is facilitated by adapting situations to their child, tend to modify their language, and accommodate their own talk to build on their children's conversations, and use topics that take account of their children's interests and abilities. Pease-Alvarez and Vasquez (1994) claim that these patterns of verbal behaviour have not been observed in some non-western and working-class communities where parents believe children learn best by adapting to their surroundings. If practitioners are aware of these differences they can plan to work with children as individuals, rather than labelling them as competent or incompetent. Assistance from parents is limited to modelling language or using cues to attract their attention, rather than scaffolding children's verbal contributions as part of a conversation.

Entering a new world: the early childhood setting

Most bicultural children have to learn English as an additional language (EAL) in order to interact in the nursery or childcare, and to assist integration into the wider community. As bicultural children move into a different context they come in contact with a variety of social and cultural influences and find themselves having to interact with adults and children from a wide variety of backgrounds and a wide variety of experiences. This contact contributes to the way they perceive themselves, their families and the place they have in it.

What happens when these children enter the new environment of the early childhood setting? Many enter an unfamiliar world where they encounter a set of language and cultural practices that may be very different from the practices they are used to. English, their second (or additional) language is likely to be the primary medium of communication. More often than not, the views and experiences of the children have not been experienced by the staff who are most likely to be white, middle-class and English-speaking. In some early years settings, adults tend to do most of the talking and their talk often focuses on a predetermined and often decontextualized (from the child's culture and experience) set of skills and topics. This bears little resemblance to the mode of talk that the children have been used to in the home. Often questions to the children focus on information that the learner does not have.

Based on her research into young bilingual children in the nursery, Drury (1997: 69) describes the early experiences of a young child (Nazma) entering the nursery. Nazma has had all her early experiences at home using her mother tongue. However, when she enters the nursery, there is an abrupt change in both cultural and language expectations. In an English language environment, Nazma is effectively dispossesed of her ability to communicate and the effect of this on a 4-year-old can be very disturbing. A number of researchers (Pease-Alvarez and Vasquez 1994; Clarke 1996; Drury 1997; Tabors 1997) argue that children like Nazma need support for their early socialization experiences as they move into new contexts.

How can we offer support?

It is important to understand the experiences that children have had prior to entry into the setting. These experiences can affect the learning outcomes of young children and include:

- family childrearing practices;
- ethnic background;
- family values, attitudes and expectations;
- immigration or refugee experiences;
- family mobility and stability;
- educational background of parents and other family members;
- language and literacy backgrounds of the parents;
- social class and economic status;
- religious / cultural beliefs;
- individual abilities;
- previous nursery / childcare or schooling;
- individual learning styles;
- play preferences;
- motivational factors;
- child's age and emotional maturity;
- gender.

(adapted from Early Literacy and the ESL Learner. Language Australia and Department of Education Training and Employment 1998. Melb, Aus.)

Pease-Alvarez and Vasquez (1994), Clarke (1996) and Drury (1997) emphasize that staff build on the existing skills and knowledge that all children bring to the school in order to maximize the connection between language and culture. Research (Clarke 1996) has shown that children's success in learning English as a second language can be facilitated by a programme which builds on the children's prior knowledge and experiences. This curriculum should deliberately reinforce their mother tongue in a bilingual programme; encourage the daily use of the children's first languages by staff and peers; incorporate the children's culture into the programme; provide bilingual and multicultural resources; and encourage staff (who have been trained) to visit the children's homes.

All those working with young children need to learn about the family and community lives of the children they teach. They can keep contact with the families, with community centres, with ethnic associations and community based organizations. They can discuss with parents and community members issues which concern both parents and staff. The following list covers some of the aspects of family and community life which should be explored and so enhance understanding.

Family history

Check on how much information you have about the family background:

- country of origin;
- length of time in new country, if appropriate;
- differences in lifestyles between the country of origin and the new country;
- members of the family;
- refugee experiences;
- previous work experiences;
- make-up of the family, for example, single parent, gay household, extended family.

Religious beliefs and practices (including important cultural events)

- special cultural and family events;
- religious observances;
- diet and food preferences;
- special religious languages (for example, Arabic).

Children's everyday life at home

- daily experiences for children;
- activities shared with children;
- participation in other activities (music, ethnic school, religion);
- routines of eating, sleeping and play.

Language practices

- literacy traditions;
- special stories and oral language practices with children;
- kinds of things talked about with children.

Parents' theories about learning

- ways children learn;
- kinds of experiences which assist children to learn;
- ways of helping children to learn;
- educational experiences with other family members;
- expectations of the teacher to help the child learn.

Parents' views on schooling and early education (also discussed later)

- knowledge of the type of schooling in this country;
- views on the type of education here;
- comparison of schooling here and in the country of origin;
- concerns about the education your child is receiving.

Community events and contacts

- special community events participated in;
- knowledge of events in the community;
- information about community services (health, medical, social security).

Areas of expertise

- hobbies;
- spare time activities;
- participation in the early childhood programme/governance;
- reading to children, music, singing, cooking, gardening.

Parents and parent involvement

Research on pre-school education in five countries evaluated by Sylva and Siraj-Blatchford (1995) for UNESCO considers the links between home and school. The authors report the importance of involving parents and the local community in the construction and implementation of the curriculum. When they begin school or early childhood education, children and their parents 'bring to the school a wealth of cultural, linguistic and economic experience which the school can call upon' (1995: 37). Sylva and Siraj-Blatchford conclude that, 'It therefore becomes the responsibility of the teacher to localise the curriculum and to enlist the support of the local community and families in framing school policy and practice and making the school and educational materials familiar and relevant to the children's experience' (1995: 37).

Parents need to be given information about the curriculum and learning outcomes and about the achievement of their children. Sharing information of this kind demands a shared understanding of what children are learning. Early years practitioners will need to establish a dialogue with parents that is meaningful to them. Observations of children can be exchanged between staff and parents in an informal way, and showing any assessments that have been done as part of the routine record keeping processes can provide a more formal means of developing mutual understandings (Moriarty and Siraj-Blatchford 1998). We suggested many practical ways of doing this in Chapter 3.

What constitutes a real partnership between parents and staff, and what increases involvement in diverse early childhood settings? According to Pugh and D'Ath (1989) partnership means 'A working relationship that is characterised by a shared sense of purpose, mutual respect and the willingness to negotiate. This implies a sharing of information, responsibility, skills, decision-making and accountability' (1989: 33).

Of course, when we talk of parents in early childhood settings we are often referring mostly to mothers. This should be recognized as regrettable, and fathers, wherever possible, should be encouraged to be involved too. Role models are important and increasing the number of male childcare workers is vital (Holmes 1998; Owen et al., 1998). Reports from several early childhood settings suggest that where there is an increase in the number of male childcare staff, the involvement of fathers is also increased. However, settings without male staff also need to become proactively involved and engage fathers through the use of appropriate visual images around the setting and by prioritizing communication with fathers.

Some minority ethnic, single and working-class parents and families continue to find it difficult enough to cope with the material circumstances in which they find themselves, let alone to feel they can enter the early childhood setting and become 'involved' in their children's formal education. This is true of both minority ethnic and majority ethnic families when economic survival can be the day-to-day priority. Many parents nowadays are members of families under stress, and every family experiences some stress at some time, whether it be related to their children, their financial circumstances or their relationships. The experience of sexism, homophobia, class prejudice, racism and discrimination in employment makes such priorities even more difficult for some families. In these circumstances staff have to think through careful strategies for accepting, supporting and encouraging parents. Until parents can trust staff there is little point in expecting their active support.

Julia Gilkes (1989) in her book, *Developing Nursery Education* describes how one nursery early childhood setting worked towards gaining the trust of families in the mainly white, working-class community in Kirkby. Gilkes explains how parents were encouraged to get involved in the early childhood setting. In some cases this meant staff first supporting the parents and their children in many ways for several years before the parents felt ready to come forward. Parents had first to feel supported, helped and valued before they could reciprocate by participating in a partnership sense. Needless to say this principle applies to most early childhood settings: Parents first and foremost need to feel that the early childhood setting offers them something, such as friendship, advice, regular reports on their child's progress, support or even just a chance to have coffee and meet other parents and carers. What Gilkes (1989) is really saying is that early childhood settings have to get their ethos right. A supportive, even therapeutic, early childhood setting creates confidence in those who have a stake in it (Siraj-Blatchford, 1994a).

The UK Children Act (Volume 2, HMSO 1989) states that parents of young children have certain parental rights, which allow them to influence the quality of education and care their child receives. They should be able to acquire information about the early childhood setting, choose between early childhood settings, and modify, express views about and contribute to their child's early childhood setting. This has serious implications for parents who are not confident about their English. Staff need to ensure that they offer the whole community an equal chance to understand and use their service. If this means translating notices about the early childhood setting and putting them in areas where minority ethnic families will see them, such as in doctors' surgeries, then this should be taken as a first step to ensure initial interest.

Parents' preconceived views of education

Not all parents whose children attend early childhood settings will have had a positive experience of education themselves, and for this reason they might distrust those to whom they are entrusting their children. Parents who are unemployed, who live in rented accommodation or suffer regular interventions in their family life by social workers and other support agencies, may feel powerless and believe they have little control over their lives or in making decisions.

Practitioners, then, clearly need to take some responsibility for building confidence and for getting to know parents as people with a life history which affects their everyday actions. Some parents will certainly be confident and will have had positive experiences of education, but this cannot be assumed. Most staff will have had relatively positive experiences of education themselves, or have at least worked out the value of learning and are committed to promoting it in the lives of others.

Pugh (1987) showed, through a survey of local authority practice on guide/handbooks for parents on services for young children, that practices varied enormously. Some authorities had produced information in minority ethnic languages, but it became clear on closer inspection that the information about services was not always reaching those who needed it (Pugh 1987: 62–3). So the role of individual early childhood settings in providing information locally is absolutely vital.

In the process of providing information and establishing a partnership it is staff who must take the lead responsibility, they are the ones with the power. It may not feel that way to individual staff, particularly those who have fewer paper qualifications or are on part-time contracts, but to the parents they represent the 'establishment', with the 'voice' that counts. All staff can work towards partnership by creating an ethos of belonging to the early childhood setting, and this will be dealt with in more detail later in this chapter.

A booklet or parent guide (if required, in the appropriate community languages) can be of help in making these points clearly and succinctly. For parents who may be working or for parents who are very busy, and particularly black and minority ethnic parents, some of whom have difficulty reading and writing in English and possibly in their own language, the best way to understanding the early childhood setting may be through personal contact. This certainly applies mainly to a minority of parents, but these are the ones with whom staff should particularly be communicating. But there is no substitute for a warm and caring reception from staff at the early childhood setting.

Parent involvement in children's learning

As Lareau (1989) has suggested, the relationship between middle-class parents and education might best be seen as one of 'interconnectedness', while in the case of working-class parents and schools the relationship is better seen as one of 'separation'. Looking at class and educational attainment from this perspective effectively turns the more usual assumption of working-class parental deficit upon its head. From this perspective, parental interest in educational attainment is only indirectly related with pupil achievement. The *cause* of the underachievement of working-class children can then be seen as the result of a mismatch of expectations regarding parental interest on the part of the educators. Early childhood settings and schools expect parents to intervene in their children's education, to be proactive and demanding. When parents appear to take no interest in the child's educational progress, centres often abdicate responsibility themselves, seeing the parental attitude as the problem feature.

Research has shown that middle-class parents do intervene in their children's education, and they do this because they simply don't trust the educational and care establishments. The problem is that minority ethnic and working-class parents often put their trust in the professionals, they believe the experts know best and that they are acting in the best interests of their children. Tragically, all too often minority ethnic and working-class parents may even lower their own expectations of their children's capabilities according to a centre's, or school's reports on their child's progress. This is where the notion of combined care and education provision comes into its own. The best of our combined centres do not just wait for parents to become involved in pre-school education and care, they are extremely proactive in this respect.

Research has actually provided us with quite a lot of information about the factors associated with underachievement, yet curiously, as Sammons (1995) notes, we know rather less about the factors associated with high achievement (1995: 467). Further research is clearly needed in this area and will be particularly valuable in informing the various mentoring initiatives that are now gaining official support.

Initiatives to involve parents have ranged in intention from compensatory to the active promotion of parent rights. This chapter is more concerned with the triad of experience and involvement between staff–child–parent, as it impacts on children's learning. It goes beyond the notion that 'more parents can be brought to understand what education can do for their children and how they can work with early childhood settings' (DES 1967).

Home–school initiatives in the last two decades have been many and varied and have changed from being largely compensatory in nature to participatory and inclusive of parents, early childhood settings and children (Bastiani 1988). Parent involvement has been interpreted in a number of ways as: parents in early childhood setting, as staff at home, the promotion of home-early childhood setting links, community education, parents as governors, parents and special educational needs, local and national representation of parents (Wolfendale 1992; Siraj-Blatchford 1994b; Siraj-Blatchford and Siraj-Blatchford 1995).

Wolfendale (1983) claims that parents are their child's prime educators, that they provide:

- the 'primary' (survival) needs;
- emotional support and endorsement (secondary) needs;
- setting for personal growth;
- the environment for exploration and hypothesis testing;
- frame of reference for exploration outside the home;
- protective environment;
- opportunities for independent functioning;
- models for language, behaviour, etc.;
- transmission of knowledge and information about the world;
- arbiters of decisions and decision makers in the short and long term.

Clearly parents are indeed very important.

Some research on parent involvement in the early years of schooling, for instance studies in reading and literacy development (Hewison 1988, Spreadbury 1995), suggest that children's educational development can be enhanced with long-term positive effects. However, other researchers suggest that some forms and patterns of parental involvement can constrain and even contribute towards the reproduction of social inequalities (Brown 1994). In working with parents then, this suggests that staff require careful preparation and planning. The research needs to be looked at carefully and critically.

As has been specified above there have been a number of studies on parent involvement in children's reading progress. Researchers have sought to investigate the reasons for poor reading scores among working-class and some minority ethnic groups with a view to improve reading scores and find the strategies which are the most effective. Studies prior to the 1980s suggested that home background did relate to a child's achievement in reading scores based on factors such as socio-economic advantage, parent attitudes and family size. Hewison and Tizard (1980) studied a cohort of working-class children to find out which factors made the greatest difference in determining whether a child would learn to read. Whether the mother heard the child read regularly seemed to be much more important than the mother's competence in language, or the child's rating on an 'intelligence' test. A number of studies followed to check this finding.

Hewison (1988) confirmed these findings using an intervention study (some children had the reading programme and others did not) in a multi-racial inner-city area of London; the gains children made in reading (for those who had the programme) remained three years after the intervention. Other schemes and projects have since proliferated with largely positive outcomes, for example, Hackney PACT scheme, paired reading (Topping and Wolfendale 1985), but it was hard to determine in the latter studies the precise cause of the improvement. Other studies were less successful; for instance, Hannon (1987) conducted a study in Sheffield into white working-class children's reading achievement when parents and children were encouraged to read books together at home. Little improvement was recorded and Hannon suggests a number of reasons as to why his study was less successful than the Hewison and Tizard study. The two most interesting reasons were the different populations under study, the London children were from multi-ethnic backgrounds and there was less professional involvement in the homes of the Sheffield children. Other studies have shown that staff involvement in the home makes a positive impact in reading (Hannon and James 1990) and early learning, for example, the High/Scope study.

We accept that parents are their children's first educators. It is likely to follow that where there is some consensus and consistency between the home and a setting's approach to children's care and education, then more effective social and learning outcomes might be achieved (Epstein 1988; Schaeffer 1992). In the United States the large-scale and longitudinal studies conducted by Joyce Epstein (Epstein 1988; Brandt 1989; Epstein and Dauber 1991) offer a useful typology upon which investigations of school and early childhood practice (particularly those aimed at raising the academic achievement of pupils) and parental involvement can be explored. Five types of parent involvement are seen as important:

1 parenting skills, child development and home environment for learning;
2 communications from school to home;
3 parents as volunteers in school;
4 involvement in learning activities at home;
5 decision making, leadership and governance.

(Brandt 1989)

Recent governments have been increasingly concerned to foster parental choice and participation in the process of their children's education. Epstein and Dauber (1991) show how most educational settings are good at promoting types 2 and 3 but fail to make adequate provision and processes to achieve 1, 4 and 5. The two latter types are more highly correlated with successful parent involvement towards real partnership and towards a better education for children. Early childhood settings might want to conduct an audit of what they do under each of these headings to support and involve parents.

Strategies for improving parent involvement

The rest of this chapter is drawn from a study conducted by Siraj-Blatchford and Brooker (1998); it was funded by one London local education authority catering for a particularly diverse population. The study involved seven schools which worked with children aged 3–7 and 8–11 years, and it looked at how parent involvement could be enhanced in the early and primary years across the authority. It was useful to start with what good practice existed within the seven settings involved in the project and the efforts they had made at improvement. Numerous activities which promoted good relations with parents and encouraged parents to take an interest in their child's learning and well-being, already existed in the project settings. New initiatives were begun during the process of the project and were felt by the settings' representatives to have raised morale and enhanced the ethos of the early childhood setting significantly.

By this stage a great deal of progress had been made by the schools in the roles and perspectives of parents and staff. These school representatives agreed that some 'outside' input had been helpful to them for most effective achievement in their own school. The following recommendations are based on the research findings and current research literature on parental involvement, child achievement and improvement in an educational and care context.

Improving ethos

1 Parents are not a homogeneous group and can therefore hold different culturally conceived ideas about the role of education and the teacher. In some cultures the role of the teacher is seen as distinct and separate to the role of parenting, and staff need to take some time explaining and illustrating how the child can benefit from partnership and continuity of educational experiences across the setting and home. It is sensible for staff not to make assumptions about parents' knowledge, beliefs or experiences but to create a friendly atmosphere where parents can talk

openly about their experiences and feelings. Additionally, sufficient interest should be taken in parents as individuals, and their views and feelings should be sought on general matters pertaining to the early childhood setting and particularly to their child. This sort of interest and care fosters trust and an open and secure ambience.

2 All staff can work towards partnership by creating an ethos of belonging to the early childhood setting. This ethos can be characterized by:

- regular and effective communication;
- willingness to share information with parents about their child and the early childhood setting;
- willingness to ask parents for advice about their child and to seek their views on key issues such as curriculum, childrearing and assessment;
- working towards common goals, taking time to explain and listen carefully;
- visibly displaying a liking for parents and respect for their feelings;
- being approachable and open to negotiation;
- sharing responsibility and a willingness to work together;
- illustrating that the child is at the heart of the education provided and therefore that the care / family unit is all-important.

3 An atmosphere or ethos that encourages a sense of belonging should aim to:

- make everyone feel that they are wanted and that they have a positive role to play in the early childhood setting;
- show parents that they can always make their feelings, views and opinions known to the staff, and that these will be dealt with respectfully and seriously;
- demonstrate that the parents' diverse linguistic, family make-up, cultural and religious backgrounds are valued and seen as positive assets to the early childhood setting; and
- show that the early childhood setting is an organic part of the community it serves and so understands the concerns, aspirations and difficulties the members of that community might face.

4 A booklet or parent guide (if required, in the appropriate community languages) can make these points clearly and succinctly. Parents with particular needs, for instance, a disability like dyslexia, an addiction like alcohol, or depression and stress should be offered support through other agencies.

5 The staff can display photographs with the names of all the workers in their early childhood setting; they can inform parents of staff who are leaving and give information on new staff. Some of the day's activities

could be displayed for the parents at the start of each day. Significant events of the day could be displayed when parents come to pick up their children, and in those few minutes when parents are waiting for children or staff, staff can easily supplement the regular personal contact with casual exchanges but this is no substitute for the regular contact.

6 Parents' first impressions are critical and the environment they come into will tell them a good deal about the values held by the early childhood setting. A bright, lively environment with displays of children's work, multicultural and multilingual material and information for parents on local activities, events and support groups can make for a comforting and secure impression. It is also essential to have somebody around who can make time to listen to parents and not rush off. Parents do not always want to talk to staff, they may just want time out to have a coffee and meet and talk to other parents or use the toy library with their toddlers.

7 Providing spaces for parents and their babies and toddlers is a valuable and very welcoming service. Parents are individuals, have specific circumstances and they have varied needs. This is true also of the service, which may be restricted in what it can provide, depending upon whether it is school, a nursery centre or a combined facility, childminder or playgroup. Expertise of staff will vary considerably as will the material resources available. It is up to individual early childhood settings to optimize their facilities and expertise to provide the best service possible, and parents should be treated as top priority.

8 Most early childhood settings have parents on their governing bodies or management committees and their views will be important in evaluating parental participation. More often than not, these parents are seen as representatives of the whole parent body but this cannot be so. Early childhood settings in diverse, multiracial areas often have no minority ethnic representation. It is almost impossible to represent every parent's views, but that is no reason to avoid consultation with as many parents as possible. Staff have to find ways of communicating with the full range of parents to get a better balance of perceived parental needs across class, gender, race and disability within the community. Where the local community appears to be homogeneous (although this is very doubtful) efforts still need to be made to represent the wider community.

Partnership between parents and staff, home and early childhood setting has been part of educational discourse for almost 30 years. However, there is still little consensus over what form this partnership should take.

Strategies for improving learning through partnership

1 A centre or school policy on parent involvement that is specifically drawn up to promote pupil educational achievement is crucial. Staff usually understand how parents can support them in their work in the centre or classroom, but on the whole they seem slightly less clear about the value and variety of learning support given by parents in the home, which is where many parents are more able and willing to make a contribution. The process by which parents and staff recognize the effectiveness of each contribution may be an important step in formulating a centre policy on involvement.

2 A quality audit on current 'best practice' would help staff start their development in a positive frame of mind and also help the management to negotiate appropriate starting points, allocate resources and construct a development plan with staff (and parents). This could be undertaken using the typology taken from Epstein (Brandt 1989); see p. 103.

3 Seek advice from community leaders and specialists on how to establish effective communication with all groups but in particular with underachieving groups, such as working-class families (especially in relation to boys' education), particular minority ethnic groups, refugee families and those with little English language support.

4 Allocate a member of staff with specific responsibility for parent involvement, ideally, a senior member of staff.

5 Canvass parent views on such matters as care, routines, the curriculum and assessment more widely than that usually achieved through the governing or management body.

6 Seek parents' advice on how to improve what the service provides, in particular in relation to matters of communication from the home and to the home.

7 Where it is appropriate, home visits should be encouraged, to help parents to understand what the early childhood setting is aiming to achieve with their child and to help staff understand the home setting. Clearly this cannot be done for all children, and would not be advisable, but some children, such as those with special educational needs (particularly where early intervention is needed), from communities we know little about and those with behavioural problems might benefit especially from closer collaboration between parents and early childhood setting. This has to be handled sensitively and with due regard to teacher/support staff time and parent's privacy and family routines.

8 Seek out literature to raise staff awareness of the benefits (and some problems) associated with parent involvement.

9 Staff should understand what kind of parent involvement they want.

According to Long (1992) there are three kinds: peripheral involvement such as fundraising and photocopying; collaboration, which includes limited educational tasks such as home reading; and partnership, which is a more cooperative parent/teacher/child venture. Few early childhood settings have achieved the latter.

10 Parents should be informed of the expectations of the early childhood setting in relation to basic obligations of the parents and vice versa.

11 Workshops should be provided for parents (after consultation with them) on their own interests and development, on how children learn and 'positive parenting'. Many of the Centres of Excellence chosen by the UK Government provide this service very successfully, for example, Hillfields Nursery Centre (Coventry) and Dorothy Gardner Nursery Centre (Westminster). Parents want more knowledge about children's learning and the setting's approach to care and learning.

12 Some early childhood settings are involved in *passive* partnership with parents, i.e. they 'use' the parents who come to the early childhood setting. The early childhood settings in our study were all aiming at *active* partnership and engaging with parents for the involvement proactively. A third dimension, which has come from the project, is the strong desire for parents to collaborate with the centre's and school's aims within the home. This we have termed *distance* partnership, where early childhood settings can develop strategies and materials that assist parents to work from the home towards the goals that schools and families have for their children. Early childhood settings can explore where they fit in this passive–active-distance (PAD) model. This model emphasizes the learning dimension of parental involvement (Siraj-Blatchford and Brooker 1998).

Further reading

Bastiani, J. (ed.) (1997) *Home–School Work in Multicultural Settings*. London: David Fulton Publishers.

Pugh, G. and D'Ath, E. (1989) *Working Towards Partnership in the Early Years*. London: National Children's Bureau.

Siraj-Blatchford, I. (1994b) Some practical strategies for collaboration between parents and early years staff. *Multicultural Teaching*, 12(2): 12–17.

6

Planning and evaluating for equity and diversity

Figure 6.1 Young children need equal access to the whole curriculum

Assessing and planning for learning

In order to transmit the skills, knowledge, understandings, attitudes and feelings that we want children to learn, we need to plan, assess and evaluate both the children and the curriculum (our contribution as staff). Fisher (1998) argues for 'customized' planning for children in the setting after the initial assessments and observations have been made of the child. She goes on to say that the cycle of assessment and planning is complex and requires staff to engage in discussion about long-term planning (for weeks and months) and short-term planning (done the day or the moment before the planning is put into practice). This planning should be related to the interests, culture and language abilities of each of the children with due regard to their home background.

Fisher (1998) suggests that long-term plans help us to offer children a broad and balanced curriculum, and to do this we need a long-term vision. This is helpful for those planning for all learning, part of which is to promote equity practices. Long-term goals may include increasing interaction or developing cooperative behaviour between children. Short-term planning helps with continuity and progression, and the monitoring of this for groups and individual children. But there is also a need for individual plans for children to ensure that their particular needs are met.

All staff in the early years need to observe, record and assess the children in their group. The purpose of this is not to grade or categorize children but to get to know the group and each individual child in it. The goal is to understand the child in the context of the programme and also to understand the child in the context of the home, family and community. A profile of each child should be compiled using regular observation techniques.

According to Moriarty and Siraj-Blatchford (1998) assessment is about understanding the learning and development of children and will affect the decisions made about the activities, resources, materials and experiences that may be planned with or for the children, both as a group and as individuals. Young children in early childhood settings are diverse in their abilities, culture and experiences and our assessments must reflect these diversities and be flexible enough to allow for individuality. This being the case, evaluation and assessment must take place at different levels. Evaluation procedures should take place in the setting so that it can be ensured that interactions and the learning programme provide a learning environment based on the settings aims, values, principles and the curriculum. There must also be a form of assessment in place to monitor the learning and development of children in the setting.

The planning of the general programme and curriculum in the setting and for individual children can then be modified as a result of such evaluations and assessments. Assessment should give useful information about learning and development; this can occur routinely or be planned to address a specific issue. Assessment that focuses on the children's learning and development should focus on individual children over a period of time and take into account the context of their learning and individual differences based on gender, ability, ethnic background and language. Single observations can only provide a limited understanding and therefore a number of observations need to be built upon over a longer period of time, so that a more sophisticated understanding can be developed.

Drummond (1993) outlines three questions that should be asked by practitioners when they are assessing children:

- 'What is there to see?' – this is about how to best assess children in different contexts and engaged in diverse and varied activities, both structured and unstructured play.
- 'How best can we understand what we see?' – this refers to the interpretations practitioners make of their observations and more formal assessments.
- 'How can we use the understandings gained from assessments?' – this refers to how observations and assessments of children can be used to further their development and learning.

Hutchin (1996) states the importance of the children themselves being involved in the assessment process. 'The purpose of the assessment process is to make explicit children's achievements, celebrate their achievements with them, then help them to move forward to the next goal. Without children's involvement in the assessment process assessment becomes a judgmental activity, resulting in a one-way view of a child's achievement' (1996: 9). She goes on to argue that children's 'significant achievement' needs to be used as an assessment tool, which will develop into a Record of Achievement for each child. The knowledge gained from observing, recording and assessing children is used to develop programmes, to set appropriate goals for children and to implement the teaching–learning process. Assessment also provides information so that:

- interested parties can be kept informed – parents, administrators, other staff working with children;
- programme evaluation can occur;
- resources can be allocated.

Fisher (1998) argues that it is crucial that educators plan a curriculum from the starting point of children's current knowledge and understanding. She argues that we must differentiate between information and evidence-based planning and assessment. We should gather information from others, but evidence is based on first-hand observations of the child:

There are two ways of establishing what children already know and can do:

1 by gathering *information* from the following sources:
   - talking to parents and carers;
   - talking to others who have knowledge of the child as a learner; and
   - looking at any previous records written on the child.
2 by gathering *evidence* in the following ways:
   - observing what the child does;
   - listening to what the child says and collecting outcomes of the child's work, e.g. photographs of models, photocopies of mark making, drawings, etc.

(Fisher 1998: 16)

We recommend that staff in each setting consider the following:

Observing

Keen observation skills are among the most important tools an early childhood educator can have. Reflection is a key ingredient of observation. It is not enough to just watch what is happening but staff also need to think about the meaning of a particular behaviour. They should then document and discuss these observations with colleagues and periodically with parents and the child.

Recording

Observations of children need to be recorded. From these records, patterns sometimes emerge that would not be evident through observation and reflection alone. Staff need to decide what method of recording best suits the learners and their classrooms. Records can include anecdotal jottings throughout the day as well as systematic recording on an agreed proforma.

Planning for assessments is probably the most important part of the assessment process. It is essential to establish the purpose or purposes of assessment and to devise a well-grounded plan to ensure that data collected and analysed will produce reliable and valid results.

Assessing bilingual children

The most effective assessments in the early years are those that are embedded in the whole curriculum, and which are interwoven into the daily programme. For children learning English as an additional language, careful planning is needed to ensure that assessment procedures are equitable. Any assessment of young children should draw on:

- the cultural and linguistic background information of the children;
- the family practices in relation to gender, religion and culture;
- the languages of the home, including the languages of extended family members who have regular contact;
- the learning styles of the cultures represented;
- the attitudes and interests of children and parents;
- the family literacy practices.

The assessment should incorporate a variety of tasks which allow the children to demonstrate their competencies in a range of areas, including use of listening, drawing, making, speaking, reading and writing. The assessment should be embedded in the day-to-day practices with which children are familiar and that give them scope to demonstrate learning in multiple ways, using a variety of learning strategies and resources.

Staff assessing the English language skills should not do this in isolation from the skills and knowledge children already have in their home language. Where the nursery or school environment is very different from the home environments of children (in terms of class, culture and language), discontinuities must be recognized and allowed for. The collection and recording of information in systematic ways provides the most consistent and relevant information about the progress of children in all areas of the curriculum. Staff need to consider how they will use the information collected before they design and gather the data.

Baseline assessment

In the UK, as part of The School Curriculum and Assessment Authority (SCAA) (1996), institutions were required to 'provide the framework for planning educational activities which ensured equality of opportunity, built on children's previous experience and achievement and responded to individual needs.' These principles should inform baseline assessment. They have particular implications for bilingual children. The National Association for Language Development in the Curriculum's (NALDIC 1998: 7) document on guidelines for baseline assessment for bilingual children. They report that:

- Bilingual children do not form a homogeneous group with access to a common experience.
- Cultures are dynamic and changing and are rightly defined by their

members. These points should be recognized to avoid stereotypical assumptions.

- Bilingual children enter school with a wide range of linguistic and cultural experiences and competencies. Thus 'baseline assessment' should add additional information to that already held by nurseries and schools.

- All staff involved in the assessment of bilingual children should be clear about the two purposes of baseline assessment. The distinction between formative assessment and establishing numerical outcomes for value added purposes should be kept in mind when making, recording and reporting the assessment.

- The benefits of bilingualism should be recognised and seen as an asset. Particularly those associated with cognitive development and high achievement.

- The role of continued development of the child's home language in the development of English as an additional language should also be acknowledged.

- Assessment should take place in the child's preferred language in order to achieve an accurate profile of a child's strengths and weaknesses.

- All staff in early years settings should recognise the relevance of the development of the home language for bilingual children. They should be informed about the outcome of assessment in their home language and should take an account of this in their planning and teaching.

(from NALDIC 1998, Working paper 4: 7)

It is also important to remember that children develop at different rates. Many children who have EAL will have an English delay because they have a language in which the school cannot work, but they will catch up. Baseline assessment will build on the initial profile of each child. This will include:

- information gained from sessions with parents conducted in the parents' languages;
- information from home visits;
- information from bilingual assistants and bilingual teachers;
- observations of the children in the nursery/school setting;
- medical or special needs records (with parental consent);
- enrolment information (preferably bilingual).

It is vital to recognize that low baseline assessment scores for some bilingual children do not necessarily reflect the children's ability. Judgements made from monolingual assessments can lead to false impressions of children's ability. Diagnosis of inappropriately low expectations can result in reduced learning opportunities or mis-diagnosis of a specific learning difficulty (NALDIC 1998).

Children learning English as an additional language may have different starting points and experiences that do not match the native speakers of English. When making an assessment of bilingual children it is important to:

- use trained bilingual staff to assist and interpret between parents and with children;
- make every effort to undertake assessments in the home language/s;
- discuss assessments with bilingual staff and parents;
- develop a profile of the child's language use at home – including literacy patterns;
- consider issues of dialect, non-standard forms of the language, languages spoken by extended family in home.

Thus, wherever possible, children should be assessed in their home language as well as English. This provides a more accurate picture of the child's language development. There is clear evidence that a strong foundation in the home language can provide the basis for more satisfactory learning of additional languages.

At present in our community there are still many people who view the simultaneous learning of two languages by young children as disadvantageous to their overall development. Sometimes conflicting advice is given to staff and parents working with young bilingual learners. In some cases, the inability to speak English is seen as a language disorder or disability. In some cases bilingual children are assessed using measures of assessment that have been devised for monolingual communities. These measures often highlight errors in speech. Unfortunately, most of these professionals are monolingual and are trained in monolingual institutes using monolingual materials and assessment tools.

Wei, Miller and Dodd (1997: 3) remind us that it is very important when undertaking assessment of bilingual children:

- to always compare the language performance of bilingual children with other bilingual children who have similar language and cultural experiences. Do not make comparisons with children who speak only English;
- to understand that when children acquire a second or additional language after acquiring their first, it is normal to hear 'errors' in their speech. This is not evidence of disorder;

- to recognize that it is normal practice for bilingual children to mix two languages or change from one to another in the same sentence;
- to recognize that it is not uncommon for bilingual children to use their languages creatively and playfully;
- to recognize that if children are not given the opportunity to continue using their home languages they may lose the ability to speak them.

It is essential to use bilingual assessments to check the child's development of its first language and to be clear about the stages of second language development in order to distinguish between normal second language development and any language delay or disorder.

In some instances it may be necessary to refer children for further assessment. In this case make sure you provide the following information to the speech pathologist, medical practitioner, etc.

- background information on the child's family background;
- languages spoken at home and community, what language is spoken in the home and to whom and when, for example mother/father to child, grandparents to child, child to siblings, other members of the household;
- length of time family/child has been in the country;
- previous experiences as an immigrant, refugee, or from a war-torn country;
- permission from parents for child to be referred (gained in writing in their own language);
- length of time child has been in nursery or school;
- any efforts by staff to use the child's first language in the nursery/school;
- any information from other key personnel who have worked with the child;
- previous assessments in a culturally acceptable setting, including use of a bilingual assessment.

Parents are also entitled to know:

- whether the professional assessing their child has experience with bilingual children;
- what knowledge the professionals have of the process of language development in bilingual children;
- whether the professional has worked with bilingual co-workers or interpreters;
- how relevant the assessment tool is for bilingual children (designed for monolingual or bilingual children);
- on what basis the professional is making decisions about whether or not

the child has a problem and about the nature of the intervention that is being suggested.

(Adapted from Wei *et al*. 1997: 4)

Assessing diversity in the curriculum

All early years services should have a written policy which recognizes the diversity in every setting associated with special needs, gender, ethnicity and class. The policy should include provision for planning, resources, staffing and training, taking into account practices and employment issues which do not disadvantage any particular group.

It is recognized that we live in a multicultural society. However, this is not necessarily acknowledged by all areas of the community. Not all early years training institutions adequately prepare staff to meet the needs of children and families from diverse backgrounds.

But all staff need to be adequately trained to cope with the difficult situations that may arise because the values of parents from different cultural, racial and linguistic backgrounds may vary. These might sometimes conflict with the values of the mainstream, or from the values held by early years staff. In areas of conflict over culture, it is important to remember that human rights take precedent over cultural rights. However, where there is conflict there is always the opportunity for negotiation. For instance, some middle-class or minority ethnic parents may expect their children to learn to read as soon as they go to school. However, many of the children need time to develop oracy or other English language skills. The more we know the more there is to learn.

By valuing all languages we are validating the languages spoken by the community. This gives power back to the language user. There are more people in the world who are bilingual than monolingual. 'However, in the British education and care systems being bilingual is still too often perceived as something the children should grow out of' (Siraj-Blatchford 1994a).

We offer an environmental rating sub-scale as a self-assessment rating scale that will enable early childhood staff to assess their own centre for equity practices (Siraj-Blatchford 1998) (see pp. 119–21). Staff should complete this in each area of their setting and do this in pairs. This should then be discussed so that staff begin to negotiate that they are looking for the same thing and have the same interpretation on events. It is with this kind of practice and negotiation that staff become proficient at using this self-evaluation tool.

The rating scale is a useful tool in the process of conducting and discussing an audit of equity practices. Staff should also be critical of the tool itself and decide what might be missing or what has been helpful. The rating scale is from 1 to 7 in the areas of how sensitive a setting is to gender equity, multicultural practice and how well a setting differentiates in planning and practice for children with particular needs and for individuals. To score, 1 is the lowest and 7 is best practice. A setting must achieve everything in one category to move on to the next one to gain a higher score. If a setting scores itself 5 on most items, but not all, and all the items under 7, then the score is 6. That is, there is room for improvement and staff can discuss this. If a setting does not score anything under the items in 3 but has some or all items in 5 they cannot score a 4 because they did not achieve any aspects of 3. This might sound harsh but the practice of equity is not easy and each score is a prerequisite to better practice.

The main purpose of this self-assessment tool is to enable staff to engage in judgements about their practice in a 'safe' environment and to stimulate discussion and reflection. The scale has been used widely as part of the Effective Provision for Pre-school Education (EPPE) project based at the University of London and it has been validated on over 200 pre-school settings. It was one scale of four that were devised to explore the quality of different aspects of the curriculum. Diversity is a key aspect that helps children to access the curriculum because it ensures that everyone in a setting is valued and treated with respect.

Further reading

National Association for Language Development in the Curriculum (1998) Guidelines on Baseline Assessment for Bilingual Children. Working paper 4, London: NALDIC.

Siraj-Blatchford, I. (1994) *The Early Years: Laying the Foundations for Racial Equality*. Stoke-on-Trent: Trentham Books.

Siraj-Blatchford, I. and Siraj-Blatchford, J. (eds) (1995) *Educating the Whole Child: Cross-curricular Skills, Themes and Dimensions in the Primary Schools*. Buckingham: Open University Press.

Wei, L., Miller, N. and Dodd, B. (1997) Distinguishing communicative difference from language disorder in bilingual children, in *The Bilingual Family Newsletter*, 14(1): 3–5.

Table 6.1 A self-assessment rating scale on diversity

Diversity: Planning for individual learning needs

Inadequate 1	2	Minimal 3	4	Good 5	6	Excellent 7
1.1 All children in the setting are offered the same range of materials and activities, rather than having activities matched to their age or aptitude.		3.1 Some additional provision is made for individuals or groups with specific needs.[1]		5.1 The range of activities provided enables children of all abilities and from all backgrounds to participate in a satisfying + e.g. cognitively demanding way.[2]		7.1 The range of activities provided, together with the organization of social interaction, enables children of all abilities and backgrounds to participate at an appropriate level in both individual and common tasks.[3]
1.2 If planning occurs there is no mention of specific groups or individuals.		3.2 Some of the planning shows differentiation for particular individuals or groups, e.g. simple peg puzzles to complex jigsaws, fat paint brushes to watercolour brushes.		5.2 Day-to-day plans are drawn up with the specific aim of developing activities that will satisfy the needs of each of the children either individually or as groups.		7.2 Planning shows attention to adult participation to individual/paired/group tasks and to the range of levels at which a task or activity may be experienced.
1.3 If records are kept, they describe activities rather than the child's response or success in that activity, + e.g. ticked checklists or sampling of children's work.		3.3 Children's records indicate some awareness of how individuals have coped with activities, or of the appropriateness of activities, + e.g. 'need bilingual support', 'could only manage to count to 3'.		5.3 Children are observed regularly, and individual records are kept on their progress in different aspects of their development.		7.3 Children are observed regularly, and their progress is recorded and used to inform planning.
		3.4 Staff show some awareness of the need to support and recognize children's differences, by giving praise and public approval to children of all abilities.		5.4 Staff regularly draw attention to differences in a positive and sensitive manner.		7.4 Staff regularly draw the attention of the whole group to difference and ability in a positive way.[4]

Notes:
1 e.g. children of different ages or developmental stage, bilingual support for bilingual children, specific support for children with learning difficulties or a disability.
2 e.g. staff demonstrate in playing with children the different tasks which can be attempted with a construction toy, computer game.
3 e.g. children of different ages or aptitudes may be paired for a particular task, such as reporting on the weather, selecting stories for a group, exploring a new computer program, or an adult may focus on working with one group or activity on a particular occasion.
4 e.g. show disabled individuals or those with learning difficulties in a positive light or individual capability is celebrated, e.g. bilingualism is seen as an asset.

Table 6.1 Continued
Diversity: Multicultural education

Inadequate 1	2	Minimal 3	4	Good 5	6	Excellent 7
1.1 Books, pictures, dolls and displays show no or very little evidence of ethnic diversity in our society or the wider world.		3.1 The children sometimes play with toys and artifacts from cultures other than the ethnic majority.		5.1 Children play with an extensive range of artifacts drawn from cultures other than the ethnic majority, e.g. dressing-up clothes used in dramatic play, cooking and eating utensils.[1]		7.1 Staff develop activities with the express purpose of promoting multi-cultural understanding, e.g. attention is drawn to similarities and differences in things and people, other cultures are routinely brought into topic work, a group of Caribbean musicians is brought into the setting to perform for the children.[3]
		3.2 Books, pictures, dolls and displays show people from a variety of ethnic groups even if the images are insensitive or stereotyped, e.g. other nationalities portrayed in national dress, African shown in traditional rural setting, black dolls with white physical features.		5.2 Books, pictures, dolls and displays sometimes show people from a variety of ethnic groups in non-stereotypical roles, e.g. black and ethnic minority scientists, doctors, engineers portrayed.		7.2 The children's attention is specifically drawn to books, pictures, dolls, etc. that show black and ethnic minority people in non-stereotyped roles, therefore communicating to children the normality of ethnic minority groups/families/individuals.
				5.3 Some images/activities developed to show the children that they have a great deal in common with people from other cultural groups, e.g. stress similarities rather than only the differences.[2]		7.3 Specific activities are developed to understand difference based on race, e.g. paints are mixed to match skin tones to show the subtlety in difference.
				5.4 Staff intervene appropriately when prejudice is shown by a child or an adult within the setting.		7.4 Black and ethnic minority people are sometimes invited into the setting to work with the children and in multi-ethnic areas ethnic minority educators are employed in the centre.

Notes:
1 Drawing children's attention to rituals of life experienced in most cultures, e.g. weddings, family meal times, birth rites, etc. Images of people from different ethnic backgrounds in posters used for projects doing everyday things, e.g. visits to the park. Posters showing physical similarities, e.g. growth, children jumping.
2 Drawing children's attention to rituals, e.g. weddings, family meal times, birth rites, visits to the park, etc. physical similarities, e.g. growth, physical abilities to jump, etc.
3 Prompt question: Do you ever get the opportunity to invite people from other cultures into your setting? For what reason do you invite them? How do you promote multicultural understanding with the children?

Table 6.1 Continued
Diversity: Gender equity and awareness

Inadequate 1	2	Minimal 3	4	Good 5	6	Excellent 7
1.1 Most books, pictures, dolls and displays show gender stereotypes.		3.1 Some books, pictures and displays include images which do not conform to gender stereotypes, e.g. father looking after baby, or female police officer.		5.1 Many books, pictures and displays show men and women in non-stereotypical roles, e.g. female doctors or plumbers.		7.1 The children's attention is specifically drawn to books, pictures, dolls and displays that show males and females in non-stereotyped roles and specific activities are developed to help the children discuss gender, e.g. reading and discussing stories like the Paperbag Princess, Mrs Plug the Plumber which challenge traditional role models.
1.2 The staff ignore or encourage stereotyped gender behaviour, e.g. boys are rarely encouraged to work in the homecorner, girls are praised for looking pretty or boys for being strong.		3.2 Children's activities and behaviour sometimes cross gender stereotypes, e.g. boys cooking or caring for dolls in the home corner, girls play outside on large mobile toys.		5.2 Children are explicitly encouraged to participate in activities which cross gender boundaries, e.g. all children are expected (not forced) to join in construction and gross-motor play.		7.2 In encouraging both boys and girls to participate equally in all activities, staff are confident in discussing and challenging the stereotyped behaviours and assumptions of children.[1]
				5.3 Dressing-up clothes encourage non-stereotyped cross-gender roles, girl and boy nurses or police outfits and non-gendered clothing, e.g. cook's hat/apron, dungarees.		7.3 Male educators are employed to work with children, where this has not been possible men are sometimes invited to work in the centre with the children.

Note:
1 Prompt question for 7.2 – are there specific times when only girls or boys are allowed to do certain things?

7

Resources

Figure 7.1 Not all resources have to be expensive. Role play props aid communication
Photograph: Sally Abbott Smith

In planning the curriculum for the early years, one of the most important aspects is to consider the resources that should be used to support the children's learning. These resources should include natural materials, materials and equipment that you make yourself, resources contributed by parents and commercially available resources such as books, posters, puzzles and toys.

The following list is provided as a guide, first, to organizations that provide support for staff working with children and families from diverse backgrounds, and second, to suppliers of appropriate resources and learning materials.

Choosing story books

In Siraj-Blatchford (1994a) staff are advised to create their own checklist to select information and storybooks, along the lines of the following which are adapted from Hazareesingh *et al.* (1989):

- How well does the story line relate to the children's home backgrounds?
- Are minority ethnic characters always associated with poverty and 'primitive' living conditions?
- Are gender roles always stereotyped?
- Are the illustrations clear, colourful and large enough to make the story easy to follow?
- Is the language appropriately simple, and does it allow repetition of words?
- Does the book/story encourage the children to participate actively? The open-and-close illustrations in Rod Campbell's book, *Dear Zoo* (1987) and the 'Spot' books invite children to take an active interest.
- Does the book allow the children to gain insights into other people's emotions, cultures and experiences?
- Do the majority ethnic characters always hold the power and make the most important decisions?
- Are the minority ethnic characters in the book shown as stupid, disruptive, menacing or subservient to others in the text?
- Does the way a story is written and described help children to value each other and the linguistic, religious, cultural, gender and class backgrounds in the setting and beyond?
- Are there enough dual language books?
- Are the illustrations of minority ethnic people life-like or do they look like majority ethnic people painted black or illustrated in a caricatured way?

If staff are unhappy about a book it is not enough simply to remove it. It is worth writing to the publisher to explain why the book is unacceptable. Chapter 4 also dealt with important issues when choosing books for young children.

Posters, puzzles and toys

The Working Group Against Racism in Children's Resources (see below for address) have produced useful guides for the evaluation and selection of toys and other resources for children. This is helpful because most educators are not aware of the powerful stereotypes that are promoted through some toys. Many educational suppliers have woken up to the fact that early years educators want manipulative toys which reflect our multi-ethnic society. The same suppliers are also producing more sophisticated and better puzzles and posters. Each setting should have a resource bank of toys, posters, puzzles, maps and labelled photographs which reflect positive images of people and help the children see that their whole world is diverse and that this is the norm.

Useful organizations in the United Kingdom

Centre for Language in Primary Education
Webber Row
London SE18 8QX
0171 401 3382

Children in Scotland
5 Shandwick Place
Edinburgh EH2 4RG
0131 228 8484

The Children's Rights Office
319 City Road
London EC1V 9PY
0171 278 8222

Commission for Racial Equality
10/11 Elliot House
Allington Street
London SW1E 5EH
0171 828 7022

Early Childhood Unit, National Children's Bureau
Wakley Street
London EC1V 7QE
0171 278 9441

Early Years Trainers Anti-Racist Network (EYTARN)
PO Box 28
Wallasey, Liverpool L45 9NP
0151 639 6136

Equal Opportunities Commission
Quay Street
Manchester M3 3HN
0161 833 9244

Equality Learning Centre
356 Holloway Road
London N7 6PA
0171 700 8127
This centre is specifically directed at those looking to increase their knowledge and resources for equity. They specialize in the early years and cover all areas of inequality in depth including disability, class and gender and ethnicity.

National Early Years Network
77 Holloway Road
London N7 6PA
0171 607 9573

Positive Identity: Multicultural Resources for Young Children
PO Box 17709
London SE6 4ZQ
0181 314 0442
Positive Identity sells black, oriental, Asian and European books, dolls, puzzles and posters which are educational and fun and also help to build children's self-esteem. Positive Identity is a mobile business that is happy to visit schools, nurseries and other childcare establishments.

Save the Children
17 Grove Jane Lane
London SE5
0171 703 5400

Working Group Against Racism in Children's Resources
406 Wandsworth Road
London SW8 3LX
0171 627 4594
This is an excellent group that provides guidelines for the evaluation and selection of toys and other resources for children. Special information packs are available for students and childcare workers. The Group also provides regular training.

National Association for Language Development in the Curriculum (NALDIC)
c/o South Herts LCSC
Holywell School Site
Tolpits Lane
Watford WD1 8NT
01923 248584
Excellent range of publications, including *Guidelines for Baseline Assessment*.

For further information check with your local regional education authority.

Useful organizations in Australia

Free Kindergarten Association Multicultural Resource Centre
1st Floor 9–11 Stewart Street
Richmond
Victoria 3121
Australia
61 (3) 9 428 4471
Fax: 61 (3) 9 429 9252
Catalogue of resources is available, it is easy to order and there are specialist materials and publications dealing with issues of diversity and working with children 0–6 years of age.

Playworks (Support for children and families with disabilities)
4 Duke Street
Prahran
Victoria 3181
Australia
61 (3) 9 521 3300

Suppliers of resources supporting diversity

Acorn Percussion
Unit 34
Abbey Business Centre
Ingate Place
London SW8 3NS
0171 720 2243
Wide range of musical instruments

AMS Educational
Woodside Trading Estate
Low Lane
Leeds LS18 5NY
0113 258 0309
Distributes multicultural resources, including many produced by ILEA

Bangladesh Resource and Multicultural Book Centre
1st Floor 23–25 Hessel Street
London E1 2LD
0171 488 4243
Bengali books, dual language books, pictures, postcards, toys, musical instruments

Child's Play
112 Tooting High Street
London SW17 ORR
0181 672 6470
Educational toys, books and games

Community Insight
Pembroke Centre
Cheney Manor
Swindon SN2 2PQ
01793 512612
References for child development and equality, children's books

Ebony Eyes
10 Searson House
Newington Butts
London SE17 3AY
0171 735 2887
Black dolls, puppets, African arts and crafts

Equality Learning Centre
356 Holloway Road
London N7 6PA
0171 700 8127
Range of resources

Galt Educational
Brookefield Road
Cheadle
Cheshire SK8 2PN
0161 627 0795
Extensive range of educational resources

Guanghwa
7–9 Newport Place
London WC2 7RJ
0171 437 3737
Chinese books and artifacts, music

Joliba
47 Colston Street
Bristol BS1 5AX
0117 9253912
Toys, puppets, dolls, textiles, musical instruments from West Africa

Knock on Wood
Granary Wharf
Leeds LS1 4BR
0113 242 9146
Music, musical instruments

Letterbox Library
Unit 2D Leroy House
436 Essex Road
London N1 3QP
0171 226 1633
Non-racist, non-sexist book club with regular newsletter – catalogue available

Mantra
5 Alexandra Grove
London N12 8NU
0181 445 5123
Fiction and non-fiction, dual language books

Minority Group Support Service
Southfields South Street
Coventry CV1 5EJ
01203 226 888

Multicultural Bookshop
6–8 Hallfield Road
Bradford
West Yorkshire BD1 3RQ
01274 731 908
Wide selection of fiction and non-fiction

Neal Street East
5 Neal Street
Covent Garden
London WC2
0171 240 0135
Crafts and fabrics from around the world

NES Arnold
Ludlow Hill Road
West Bridgeford
Nottingham NG2 6HD
01159 452201
Wide range of educational equipment and multicultural resources

New Beacon Books
76 Strand Green Road
London N4 3EN
0171 272 4889
Specializing in Africa and the Caribbean

Soma Books
38 Kennington Lane
London SE11 4LS
0171 735 2101
Wide range of books, crafts, textiles from South East Asia

Sterns
293 Euston Road
London NW1
0171 387 5550
CDs and cassettes of music from around the world

Tamarind Ltd
PO Box 296
Camberley
Surrey GU1 1QW
01276 683 979
Books, puzzles promoting diversity

Trentham Books Ltd
Westview House
734 London Road
Oakhill
Stoke-on-Trent ST4 5NP
01782 745 567
Fax: 01782 745 553

Resources for music and the arts

A useful starting point is to contact your Local Authority Arts Adviser. A list of such contacts nationally is available from:

Arts Council of England
14 Great Peter Street
London SW1P 3NQ
020 7333 0100
Contact: Pax Nindi

Lists for Greater London are available from:

London Arts
2 Pear Tree Court
London EC1R 0DS
020 7608 6100

A wonderful resource for music, singing and rhythms are the CDs and cassettes of Ella Jenkins – a black American folk singer who has specialized in music for young children. These are produced by Folkways Records and can be purchased from good music outlets in the UK.

In Australia, these CDs and cassettes are available from the FKA Multicultural Resource Centre Melbourne and the Book Garden in Sydney and Brisbane. An essential resource for every early years setting.

A useful resource pack for schools is the **Lambeth Schools Carnival Pack –** *Carnival in the Curriculum*. This is available from:

Lambeth Schools Carnival Group
13 Helix Gardens
Brixton
London SW22 2JJ

Useful contacts in London:

Danny Staples (Multicultural/world music)
103 South Croxted Road
London SE21 8BA
020 8670 0270
He is a freelance education worker and specialist in music education who works a lot with young children. He is very happy to help.

World Muzik Makers
10 Banting House
Ainsworth Close
London NW2 7ED
07957 590 407
batanai@aol.com
http://members.aol.com/batanai/

Wil Joseph
Education Officer
African and Caribbean Music Circuit Ltd
Unit 8 Buspace Studios
Conlan St
London W10 5AP
020 8960 6220
music.circuit@lineone.net

Nana Appiah 'Kudum' (Focus on Ghanaian and West African Music)
07944 894 130
020 7700 1092

'Whippersnappers'
020 7274 3949
Music workshop for Early Years. Speak to Caroline.

Viv Golding
Harniman Museum Education Department
020 8699 1872 ext. 157

'Music Monkeys' (Anita and Marie)
Work with young children making musical instruments.
Contact via Harniman Museum.

Alex Pascall
Bookings: Ingrid Wilson
Telephone/Fax: 01633 267 367
Drumming, calypso, rhyme and story telling. Very experienced working in schools.

Karen Mears and Clare Baker
Indigo Art
22 Rossiter Road
London SW12 9RU
020 8675 4188
020 8678 0949
artbluetone@cs.com
Arts workshop for Early Years (Fabric, costumes, masks, etc.).

Thelma Perkins
020 8761 7202
Early Years teacher/researcher. Very experienced practitioner. Member of Caribbean Women Writers' Alliance. Has lots of contacts and resources.

'Cloth of Gold'
020 7372 0628
Runs arts workshops.

Useful journals and publications

The Bilingual Family Newsletter
Multilingual Matters Ltd
Frankfurt Lodge
Clevedon Hall
Clevedon BS21 7SJ
01275 876 519
Fax: 01275 343 096
This is an excellent publication full of useful articles and practical suggestions for raising children bilingually. The newsletter is informative and family oriented. A free sample is sent out on request.

Multicultural Teaching
Produced by Trentham Books (see p. 129)

NALDIC News
National Association for Language Development in the Curriculum (NALDIC)
c/o South Herts LCSC
Holywell School Site
Tolpits Lane
Watford WD1 8NT
This is an excellent publication which has a special 'early years' interest group. Many articles are relevant for those working with children in the 3–8 age group.

Resource

FKA Multicultural Resource Centre

1st Floor 9–11 Stewart Street

Richmond

Victoria 3121

Australia

61 (3) 9 428 4471

Fax: 61 (3) 9 429 9252

Available on subscription. This is an excellent newsletter that is published four times a year and has practical articles for staff working with issues of diversity.

Young Children

National Association for the Education of Young Children

Washington DC

An excellent journal with many relevant articles for staff working with issues of diversity.

Videos

FKA Multicultural Resource Centre

1st Floor 9–11 Stewart Street

Richmond

Victoria 3121

Australia

61 (3) 9 428 4471

Fax: 61 (3) 9 429 9252

VHS format

- *'and now English'*, 20-minute video outlining the way children 0–5 years develop English as a second language;
- *Bilingual Staff Work*, 20-minute video demonstrating the important role played by bilingual staff in children's services;
- *Journey to the Future* – a 17-minute video showing a day at a bilingual childcare centre;
- *Music Makers* – a 24-minute video promoting the importance of music for children.

Others

Early Literacy Education with Parents

Video and manual available from Sheffield University Television

5 Favell Road

Sheffield S3 7QX

Educating the Whole Child
Equality Learning Centre
356 Holloway Road
London N7A 6PA
0171 700 8127

References

Almy, M. (1988) *The Child's Right to Play*. Berkeley, CA: University of California Press.

Am, E. (1986) Play in the preschool – some aspects of the role of the adult. *International Journal of Early Childhood*, 18(2): 90–7.

Bastiani, J. (1988) (ed.) *Parents and Staff 2 – From Policy to Practice*. Slough: NFER-Nelson.

Bernstein, B. (1992*)* *The Structuring of Pedagogic Discourse: Volume IV, Class, Codes and Control*. London: Routledge.

Brandt, R. (1989) On parents and early childhood settings: a conversation with Joyce Epstein. *Educational Researcher*, 14: 3–10.

Bredekamp, S. (ed.) (1987) *Developmentally Appropriate Practice in Early Childhood Programs Serving Children from Birth Through Age 8*. Washington, DC: National Association For the Education of Young Children.

Brown, A. (1994) Exploring dialogue between staff and parents: a sociological analysis of IMPACT diaries. Unpublished paper, Institute of Education, University of London.

Brown, B. (1998) *Unlearning Discrimination in the Early Years*. Stoke-on-Trent: Trentham Books.

Bruner, J.S. (1975) The ontogenesis of speech acts. *Journal of Child Language*, 2: 1–19.

Bruner, J.S. (1983) *Child's Talk: Learning to Use Language*. Oxford: Oxford University Press.

Bruner, J.S. (1990a) Culture and human development: a new look. *Human Development*, 33: 344–55.

Bruner, J.S. (1990b) *Acts of Meaning*. Cambridge, MA: Harvard University Press.

Bruner, J.S. and Sherwood, V. (1981) Peekaboo and the learning of rule structures, in J.S. Bruner, A. Jolly and K. Sylva (eds) *Play: Its Role in Development and Evolution*, New York: Basic Books.

Campbell, R. (1987) *Dear Zoo*. London: Ingham Yates.

Carle, E. (1969) *The Very Hungry Caterpillar*. London: Jonathan Cape.

Celestin, N. (1986) *A Guide to Anti-racist Child Care Practice*. London: Voluntary Organisations Liaison Council for Under-fives.

Clarke, P. (1976) An exploration study of the interaction between children and a variety of listeners: To what extent do children vary their speech when communicating with adults, peers and younger children. Unpublished study, Latrobe University.

Clarke, P. (1991) Does your program support the development of English as a 2nd language. *Resource*. Newsletter of the FKA Multicultural Resource Centre. Issue 67.

Clarke, P. (1993) Multicultural perspectives in early childhood services in Australia, *Multicultural Teaching*, Stoke-on-Trent: Trentham Books.

Clarke, P. (1996) Investigating second language acquisition in preschools: a longitudinal study of four Vietnamese-speaking four-year-olds' acquisition of English. Unpublished PhD thesis, LaTrobe University, Melbourne, Victoria.

Clarke, P. (1997) Principles of second language learning. Unpublished paper. Melbourne, Victoria: FKA Multicultural Resource Centre.

Clarke, P. (1999) Supporting bilingual learners. Workshop Papers. Melbourne, Victoria: Free Kindergarten Association.

Clarke, P. and Milne, R. (1996) Maintaining the first language and learning English as a 2nd language. In *Book of Readings*, Melbourne, Victoria: FKA Multicultural Resource Centre.

Cockram, L. and Cook, C. (1994) Settling in – a process not an event. *Resource*, Newsletter of the FKA Multicultural Resource Centre. 80, August.

Cook, C. and Porter, C. (1996) *Babies and Toddlers: Considering Multicultural Perspectives*. Victoria: FKA Multicultural Resource Centre.

Creaser, B.H. (1989) An examination of the four-year-old master dramatist. *International Journal of Early Childhood*, 21(2): 55–65.

Davey, A. (1983) *Learning to be Prejudiced*. London: Edward Arnold.

Davies, B. (1989) *Frogs and Snails and Feminist Tales*. St Leonards, NSW: Allen & Unwin.

Department of Education and Science (DES) (1967) *The Plowden Report*. London: HMSO.

Department of Education and Science (DES) (1985) *Education for All, The Swann Report*, London: HMSO.

Derman-Sparks, L. (1992) Reaching potentials through antibias, multicultural curriculum, in S. Bredekamp and T. Rosengrant (eds) *Reaching Potentials: Appropriate Curriculum and Assessment for Young Children*, 1: 114–27. Washington DC: NAEYC.

Directorate of School Education (1992) ESL Essentials. Junior Primary ALTA Beginner Stages. Victoria, Aus.

Drummond, M.J. (1993) *Assessing Children's Learning*. London: David Fulton.

Drury, R. (1997) Bilingual children in the preschool years, in C. Leung and C. Cable (eds) *English as an Additional Language*. London: NALDIC.

Dulay, H., Burt, M. and Krashen, S. (1982) *Language Two*. New York: Oxford University Press.

Dunn, J. (1987) Understanding feelings: the early stages, in J. Bruner and H. Haste (eds) *Making Sense: The Child's Construction of the World*, pp. 26–40. London: Routledge.

Dweck, C.S. and Leggett, E. (1988) A social-cognitive approach to motivation and personality. *Psychological Review*, 95(2): 256–73.

Early Childhood Education Forum (ECEF) (1998) *Quality in Diversity in Early Learning: A Framework for Early Childhood Practitioners*, London: National Children's Bureau.

Elliott, J. (1994) Scaffolding learning. *Every Child*, 1(2): 8–9. Melbourne: Australian Early Childhood Association.

Epstein, J. (1988) Effective schools or effective students? Dealing with diversity, in R. Haskins and D. MacRae (eds) *Policies for America's Public Schools: Staff, Equity and Indicators*, pp. 89–126. Norwood, NJ: Ablex.

Epstein, J.L. and Dauber, S.L. (1991) Schools programs and staff practices of parent involvement in inner-city elementary and middle schools. *The Elementary School Journal*, 91(3): 289–305.

Erikson, E.H. (1950) *Childhood and Society*. New York: W.W. Norton.

Fisher, J. (1998) The relationship between planning and assessment, in Siraj-Blatchford, I. (1998) (ed) *A Curriculum Development Handbook for Early Childhood Educators*, pp. 15–44. Stoke-on-Trent: Trentham Books.

Fleer, M. (1999) Universal fantasy: the domination of western theories of play, in E. Dau (ed.) *Child's Play: Revisiting Play in Early Childhood Settings*, pp. 67–80. Sydney: Maclennan and Petty.

Fraser, S. and Wakefield, P. (1986) Fostering second language development through play in a multilingual classroom, *TESL Canada Journal/Revue TESL du Canada*. Special issue, (1): 19–27.

Gardner, H. (1991) *Frames of Mind*. New York: Basic Books.

Gilkes, J. (1989) *Developing Nursery Education*. Milton Keynes: Open University Press.

Gillborn, D. (1990) *Race, Ethnicity and Education*. London: Unwin Hyman.

Gillborn, D. and Gipps, C. (1997) *Recent Research on the Achievements of Minority Ethnic Pupils*. London: HMSO.

Gonzales-Mena, J. (1993) *Multicultural Issues in Child Care*. Mountain View, CA: Mayfield Publishing.

Gonzales-Mena, J. (1998) *Foundations: Early Childhood Education in a Diverse Society*, Mountain View, CA: Mayfield Publishing.

Grossberg, L. (1994) Introduction: bringing it all back home – pedagogy and cultural studies, in H. Giroux and P. McLaren (eds) *Between Borders: Pedagogy and the Politics of Cultural Studies*, pp. 1–28. London: Routledge.

Grugeon, E. and Woods, P. (1990) *Educating All: Multicultural Perspectives in the Primary School*. London: Routledge.

Hakuta, K. (1986) *Mirror of Language: The Debate on Bilingualism*. New York: Basic Books.

Hakuta, K. and Pease-Alvarez, L. (1992) Enriching our views of bilingualism and bilingual education. *Educational Researcher*, 21: 4–6.

Hall, S. (1992) Race, culture and communications: looking backward and forward in cultural studies, in *Rethinking Marxism*, 5: 10–18.

Hannon, P. and James, A. (1990) Parents' and staff perspectives on pre-school literacy development. *British Educational Research Journal*, 16(3): 91–111.

Hannon, P. (1987) A study of the effects of parental involvement in the teaching of reading on children's reading test performance. *British Journal of Educational Psychology*, 57: 56–72.

Hazareesingh, S., Simms, K. and Anderson, P. (1989) *Educating the Whole Child*. London: Save the Children.

Heath, S.B. (1982) Questioning at home and at school: a comparative study, in G. Spindler (ed.) *Doing the Ethnography of Schooling*, pp. 102–31. New York: Holt, Rinehart and Winston.

Heath, S.B. (1983) *Ways with Words: Language, Life and Work in Communities and Classrooms*. Cambridge: Cambridge University Press.

Hewison, J. and Tizard, B. (1980) Parental involvement and reading attainment. *British Journal of Educational Psychology*, 50: 209–15.

Hewison, J. (1988) The long term effectiveness of parental involvement in reading: a follow-up study to the Haringey reading project. *British Journal of Educational Psychology*, 58: 184–90.

Holmes, R. (1998) Breaking the mould: men in early childhood services. *Community Quarterly Journal*, 46: 17–20.

Hurst, V. and Joseph, J. (1998) *Supporting Early Learning: The Way Forward*. Buckingham: Open University Press.

Hutchin, V. (1996) *Tracking Significant Achievement in the Early Years*. London: Hodder and Stoughton.

Jalongo, M.R. (1996) Teaching young children to become better listeners. *Young Children*, 51(2): 21–6.

Kesslar, C. and Quinn, M. (1982) Cognitive development in bilingual environments, in A. Valdman and R. Foster (eds) *Issues in International Bilingual Education: The Role of the Vernacular*. New York: Plenum Press.

Kesslar, C. and Quinn, M. (1987) Language minority children's linguistic and cognitive creativity. *Journal of Multilingual and Multicultural Development*, 8(1): 173–86.

Lang, P. (1995) The place of PSE in the primary school, in I. Siraj-Blatchford and J. Siraj-Blatchford (eds) *Educating the Whole Child: Cross-curricular Skills, Themes and Dimensions in the Primary Schools*. Buckingham: Open University Press.

Language Australia and Department of Education Training and Employment (1998) Early Literacy and the ESL Learner. Melb, Aus.

Lareau, A. (1989) *Home Advantage: Social Class and Parental Intervention in Elementary Education*. London: Falmer Press.

Lawrence, D. (1988) *Enhancing Self-esteem in the Classroom*. London: Paul Chapman.

Lightbown, P. and Spada, N. (1995) *How Languages are Learned*. Oxford: Oxford University Press.

Lloyd, B. (1987) Social representations of gender, in J. Bruner and H. Haste (eds) *Making Sense: The Child's Construction of the World*, pp. 147–62. London: Routledge.

Lloyd, B. and Duveen, G. (1992) *Gender Identities and Education*. London: Harvester Wheatsheaf.

Long, R. (1992) Parent involvement or parent compliance? Parental roles and school improvement, in *Ruling the Margins: Problematising Parental Involvement*, conference paper, University of North London in association with the Institute of Education, University of London.

Lubeck, S. (1996) The politics of developmentally appropriate practice, in B.L. Mallory and R.S. New (eds) *Diversity and Developmentally Appropriate Practices: Challenges for Early Childhood Education*. New York: Teachers College Press.

MacNaughton, G. (1999) Even pink tents have glass ceilings: crossing the gender boundaries in pretend play, in E. Dau (ed.) *Child's Play: Revisiting Play in Early Childhood Settings*, pp. 81–96. Sydney: Maclennan and Petty.

MacPherson, W. (1999) *Report of the Stephen Lawrence Enquiry*. London: HMSO.

Mahony, P. (1985) *Schools for the Boys*. London: Hutchinson.

Makin, L., Campbell, J. and Jones Diaz, C. (1995) *One Childhood Many Languages*. Sydney: Harper Educational.

McKay, P. and Scarino, A. (1991) *ESL Framework of Stages: An Approach to ESL Learning in Schools, K–12*. Carlton: Curriculum Corporation.

Milne, R. (1990) About reading. *Resource*. Newsletter of the FKA Multicultural Resource Centre, Issue 64, Melbourne.

Milne, R. (1993) Being an infant, toddler or two-year-old; remember what it feels like. *Resource*. Newsletter of the FKA Multicultural Resource Centre, Issue 75, Melbourne.

Milne, R. (1997) *Marketing Play*. Melbourne, Victoria: Free Kindergarten Association.

Milne, R. and Clarke, P. (1993) *Bilingual Education in Child Care and Preschool Centres*. Melbourne, Victoria: FKA Multicultural Resource Centre.

Milne, R. and Clarke, P. (1995) *Maintaining the First Language*, booklet and pamphlets for staff and parents. Melbourne, Victoria: FKA Multicultural Resource Centre.

Milner, D. (1983) *Children and Race: Ten Years On*. London: Ward Lock Educational.

Moriarty, V. and Siraj-Blatchford, I. (1998) *An Introduction to Curriculum for 3 to 5-Year-Olds*. Nottingham: Education Now Books.

National Association for Language Development in the Curriculum (1998) Guidelines on baseline assessment for bilingual children. Working paper No 4, London: NALDIC.

Nemoianu, A.M. (1980) *The Boat's Gonna Leave: A Study of Children Learning a Second Language from Conversations with Other Children*. Amsterdam: John Benjamins BV.

Neugebauer, B. (1992) *Alike and Different: Exploring our Humanity with Young Children*. Washington, DC: NAEYC.

Owen, C., Cameron, C. and Moss, P. (1998) (eds) *Men as Workers in Services for Young Children: Issues of a Mixed Gender Workforce*. London: Institute of Education.

Pease-Alvarez, C. and Vasquez, O. (1994) Language socialization in minority ethnic communities, in F. Genesee (ed.) *Educating Second Language Children: The Whole Child, the Whole Curriculum, the Whole Community.* Cambridge: Cambridge University Press.

Philips, S. (1972) Participant structures and communicative competence: Warm Springs children in community and classroom, in V. John, C. Cazden and D. Hymes (eds) *Functions of Language in the Classroom.* Prospect Heights, IL: Waveland Press.

Philips, S. (1983) *The Invisible Culture: Communication in Classroom and Community on the Warm Springs Indian Reservation.* New York: Longman.

Piaget, J. (1962) *Play, Dreams and Imitation in Childhood.* New York: W.W. Norton.

Pugh, G. (1987) *Partnership in Action: Working with Parents in Pre-school Centres.* London: National Children's Bureau.

Pugh, G. and D'Ath, E. (1989) *Working Towards Partnership in the Early Years.* London: National Children's Bureau.

Purkey, W. (1970) *Self-concept and School Achievement.* London: Paul Chapman.

Ratner, N. and Bruner, J. (1978) Games, social exchange and the acquisition of language. *Journal of Child Language*, 5: 391–401.

Roberts, R. (1998) Thinking about me and them: personal and social development, in I. Siraj-Blatchford (ed.) *A Curriculum Development Handbook for Early Childhood Educators*, pp. 155–74. Stoke-on-Trent: Trentham Books.

Rogers, C.S. and Sawyers, J.K. (1988) *Play in the Lives of Children.* Washington, DC: NAEYC.

Ross, C. and Ryan, A. (1990) *'Can I Stay in Today Miss?' Improving the School Playground.* Stoke-on-Trent: Trentham Books.

Sammons, P. (1995) Gender, ethnic and socio-economic differences in attainment and progress: a longitudinal analysis of student achievement over nine years. *British Education Research Journal*, 21(4): 465–85.

School Curriculum and Assessment Authority (SCAA) (1996) *Nursery Education: Desirable Outcomes for Children's Learning on Entering Compulsory Education.* London: SCAA and DfEE.

Schieffelin, B.B. and Ochs, E. (1986) Language socialization. *Annual Review of Anthropology*, 15: 163–246.

Schofield, J. (1982) *Black and White in School: Trust, Tension or Tolerance.* New York: Praeger.

Schrader, C. (1990) Symbolic play as a curricular tool for early literacy development. *Early Childhood Research Quarterly*, 5: 79–103.

Sebastian-Nickell, P. and Milne, R. (1992) *Care and Education of Young Children.* Melbourne, Victoria: Longman.

Schaeffer, S. (1992) Collaborating for educational change: the role of parents and the community in school improvement. *International Journal of Educational Development*, 12(4): 277–95.

Siraj-Blatchford, I. (1992) Why understanding cultural differences is not enough, in G. Pugh (ed.) *Contemporary Issues in the Early Years.* London: Paul Chapman Publishers.

Siraj-Blatchford, I. (1994a) *The Early Years: Laying the Foundations for Racial Equality.* Stoke-on-Trent: Trentham Books.

Siraj-Blatchford, I. (1994b) Some practical strategies for collaboration between parents and early years staff. *Multicultural Teaching,* 12(2): 12–17.

Siraj-Blatchford, I. (1996) Language, Culture and Difference, in C. Nutbrown *Children's Rights and Early Education,* pp. 23–33. London: Paul Chapman.

Siraj-Blatchford, I. (1998) (ed.) *A Curriculum Development Handbook for Early Childhood Educators.* Stoke-on-Trent: Trentham Books.

Siraj-Blatchford, I. and Brooker, L. (1998) Parent Involvement Project in One London LEA – Research Report, University of London, Institute of Education.

Siraj-Blatchford, I. and Siraj-Blatchford, J. (1999) Race, research and reform: the impact of the three Rs on anti-racist pre-school and primary education in the UK. *Race, Ethnicity and Education,* 2(1): 127–48.

Siraj-Blatchford, J. and Siraj-Blatchford, I. (eds) (1995) *Educating the Whole Child: Cross-curricular Skills, Themes and Dimensions in the Primary Schools.* Buckingham: Open University Press.

Siraj-Blatchford, J. and McLeod-Brudenell, I. (1999) *Supporting Science, Design and Technology in the Early Years.* Buckingham: Open University Press.

Skutnabb-Kangas, T. (1981) *Bilingualism or Not: The Education of Minorities.* Clevedon, England: Multilingual Matters Ltd.

Spreadbury, J. (1995) Why parents read to children. *Australian Journal of Early Childhood,* 20(1).

Stonehouse, A. (1991) *Opening the Doors: Childcare in a Multicultural Society.* Melbourne, Victoria: Australian Early Childhood Association Inc.

Suschitzky, W. and Chapman, J. (1998) *Valued Children, Informed Teaching.* Buckingham: Open University Press.

Sylva, K. and Siraj-Blatchford, I. (1995) *The Early Learning Experiences of Children 0–6: Strengthening Primary Education Through Bridging the Gap between Home and School.* Paris: UNESCO.

Tabors, P.O. (1997) *One Child, Two Languages: A Guide for Preschool Educators of Children Learning English as a Second Language.* Baltimore, MD: Paul Brookes Publishing.

Topping, K. and Wolfendale, S. (1985) *Parental Involvement in Children's Reading.* London: Croom Helm.

Trevarthen, C. (1992) An infant's motives for thinking and speaking in the culture, in A.H. Wold (ed.) *The Dialogical Alternative,* pp. 99–137. Oxford: Oxford University Press.

Troyna, B. and Hatcher, R. (1991) *Racism in Children's Lives: A Study of Mainly White Primary Schools.* London: National Children's Bureau and Routledge.

United Nations (1989) *The Convention on the Rights of the Child.* Defence for Children International and the United Nations Children's Fund, Geneva, p. 16.

Vygotsky, L. (1962) *Thought and Language.* Cambridge, MA: MIT Press.

Vygotsky, L. (1978) *Mind in Society.* Cambridge, MA: Harvard University Press.

Walkerdine, V. (1987) Sex, power and pedagogy, in M. Arnot and G. Weiner (eds) *Gender and the Politics of Schooling,* pp. 166–74. London: Unwin Hyman.

Wardle, F. (1999) *Tomorow's Children: Meeting the Needs of Multiracial and Multiethnic*

Children at Home, in Early Childhood Programs and at School, Denver, CO: Center for the Study of Biracial Children.

Wei, L., Miller, N. and Dodd, B. (1997) Distinguishing communicative difference from language disorder in bilingual children. *The Bilingual Family Newsletter*, 14(1): 3–5.

Wells, G. (ed.) (1981) *Learning Through Interaction*. Cambridge: Cambridge University Press.

Willett, J. (1987) Contrasting acculturation patterns of two non–English speaking preschoolers, in H. Trueba (ed.) *Success or Failure: Learning and the Language Minority Student*, pp. 69–84. New York: Newbury House.

Willis, P. (1977) *Learning to Labour*. London: Saxon House.

Wolfendale, S. (1983) *Parents in the Education and Development of Children*. London: Gordon and Breach.

Wolfendale, S. (1992) *Empowering Parents and Staff*. London: Cassell.

Wong-Fillmore, L. (1976) The second time around: cognitive and social strategies in second language acquisition. PhD dissertation, Stanford, CA: Stanford University.

Wong-Fillmore, L. (1991) When learning a second language means losing the first. *Early Childhood Research Quarterly*, 6: 323–47.

Index

PROMOTING CHILDREN'S LEARNING FROM BIRTH TO FIVE
DEVELOPING THE NEW EARLY YEARS PROFESSIONAL

Angela Anning and Anne Edwards

- What sort of literacy and numeracy curriculum experiences are best suited to the needs of very young children?
- How can early years professionals bridge the current divisions between education and care to provide an approach to young children's learning which draws on the strengths of both traditions?
- How can these professionals be supported as they develop new practices which focus on young children as learners?
- What strategies are most effective in involving parents with their children's development in literacy and mathematical thinking?

Drawing upon research carried out in a range of early years settings, Angela Anning and Anne Edwards seek to address these questions. The emphasis throughout is upon enhancing the quality of children's learning and providing support for the practitioners who work with them. The complexity of addressing the various cognitive, social, physical and emotional learning needs of young children is discussed and practical strategies to develop children's learning are explored with a particular focus on communication and mathematical thinking. Published at a time of dramatic change in pre-school provision in the UK, the book will both inform and reassure early childhood professionals. It will be important reading for managers, administrators and all professionals working in early years and family services and an accessible text for those studying for childcare and education, and teaching qualifications.

Contents

Introduction – Setting the national scene – Integration of early childhood services – The inquiring professional – Young children as learners – Language and literacy learning – How adults support children's literacy learning – Mathematical learning – How adults support children's mathematical thinking – Creating contexts for professional development in educare – Early childhood services in the new millennium – Bibliography – Author index – Subject index.

192 pp   0 335 20216 0 (paperback)   0 335 20217 9 (hardback)